HARVESTING NEW
GENERATIONS

HARVESTING NEW GENERATIONS:

THE POSITIVE DEVELOPMENT OF BLACK YOUTH

by Useni Eugene Perkins

Third World Press   Chicago

First Edition, Third Printing
ISBN 0-88378 -116-6 (paper)

Manufactured in the United States of America

Third World Press • Chicago
7524 S. Cottage Grove Ave.
Chicago, IL 60619

Cover illustration by Larry Crowe

Other Books by Useni Eugene Perkins

Sociology
Home Is A Dirty Street: The Social Oppression of Black Children
Explosion of Chicago's Black Street Gangs
The Afrocentric Self-Inventory and Discovery Workbook

Poetry
An Apology to My African Brother
Silhouette
Black Is Beautiful
The West Wall
When You Grow Up
Midnight Blues In The Afternoon

Dedicated to my children,
   Julia Evalyn, Russell Patrice and Jamila Saran;
and to Steve Goosby.

▰▰▰▰▰ TABLE OF CONTENTS ▰▰▰▰▰

PREFACE

The status of today's Black youth has become a topic steeped in controversy and pessimism. Indeed, it has aroused some people to proclaim that Black youth are being programmed for failure and fastly becoming "an endangered species." Others comment that Black youth have been woefully neglected and literally left to survive on their own. These perceptions are graphically reinforced when one observes the disproportionate number of Black youth who are locked in the juvenile justice system, hooked on drugs and alcohol, disenchanted with school, alienated from their parents, and disenfranchised from legitimate opportunities to gain meaningful employment. And even those Black youth who do not fall into any of these categories appear to be misguided in their values and show little commitment to the Black community. This perception is evidenced by the increasing number of Black students, known as bumpies, who massage their egos through self adulation and adopt values supposedly void of any racial references. In addition, the escalation among Black youth in teenage pregnancies, mental illness and homicides/suicides, and the high risks associated with single parent families leave many with questionable futures. Finally, to compound all of these problems, Black youth must learn to cope with the perils of being Black in a white racist society that plays Russian roulette with their lives.

In an earlier book, *Home Is A Dirty Street: The Social Oppression of Black Children*, I identified many of these problems as being caused by the system of oppression that creates the Ghetcolony—a term used to describe the so-called Black ghetto. To survive this system, Black youth find refuge in the Street Institution where they learn to live under prescribed norms and values taught by adults whose lifestyles are often self-defeating. As a result, the Street Institution and its collaboratives play an important role in the socialization of Black youth. Obviously, if we are to change the debilitating status of Black youth, it appears logical that we, first, examine and change the pattern of socialization that stymies and inhibits their positive development. So long as we allow white America to define and control the socialization of Black youth, they will be harnessed to a cyclical form of oppression that takes its toll on each new generation.

This commentary is an attempt to analyze the systematic causes that impair the positive development of Black youth and provide solutions to them. More specifically, it advocates the cultivation of a "new harvest" that can provide future generations of Black youth with a greater opportunity to achieve their true potential. Furthermore, I recommend that the socialization of Black youth be processed through a "Rites of Passage" based on the principles of Afrocentricity. In the institutionalization of this model, we will be able to reap a harvest which will blossom for generations yet to come.

In the preparation of this commentary, I'm indebted to many people who have inspired me over the years and in some way have contributed to my own development. Among these are my deceased parents, Marion and Eva Perkins, Margaret Burroughs, Fern Gayden, Lerone Bennett, Jr., Hannibal Tirus Afrik, Bobby Wright (deceased), and my spiritual ancestor, Paul Robeson. Finally, I would like to give special thanks to my friend and publisher, Haki Madhubuti, Diane Glenn who typed the drafts, and Margo Crawford who edited and prepared the final manuscript; to my dear brother, Toussaint, for his expressive illustrations, and to members of my extended family, the Catalyst, who have helped me through my own belated "Rites of Passage."

Useni Eugene Perkins
August 18, 1985

✖✖✖✖✖✖✖ INTRODUCTION ✖✖✖✖✖✖✖

European slavery of African people drew a dark cloud across the sky and caused massive atmospheric pollution that contaminated the human arena. This lethal cloud of greed and human bondage etched a line across the world dividing it between the slave and the master, the human and non-human, the developed and underdeveloped, the colonized and settler, the first and third worlds. The victims of this system of violence and human degradation are always affixed in an isolated place, locked in, boxed in behind a wall, shielded from the rays of freedom, opportunity, equality, hope, and the maximization of human possibility.

The great abolitionist and orator, Frederick Douglass, wisely called western slavery "a hideous monster that is a curse to the earth that supports it."[1] Dr. W.E.B. DuBois, in his prophetic wisdom, appropriately called the black side of the line a prison and declared that the tensions generated by its existence would be the agenda for the 20th century. In his seminal work, *The Souls of Black Folk*, he proclaimed: "The problem of the twentieth century is the problem of the color-line—the relation of the darker to the lighter races of men in Asia and Africa, in America and the islands of the sea."[2] He understood the inimical impact that this partition has upon the integrity of those of us who are black, that it grants to us no true identity, but only a struggle of double consciousness. More dastardly, it insidiously exposes us to the amuse contempt of those on the other side of the line.

The Black poet, Claude McKay, named the black side of the line "an inglorious spot"[3] with white America making its mock of our accused lot. Forty years hence, Dr. Kenneth Clark referred to this "inglorious spot" as a *Dark Ghetto*,[4] an economic and political colony that serves to denigrate those entrapped.

Dr. Howard Thurman reminds us that the walls that imprison us are as exhilarating as they are debilitating. He recognized that our ability to adapt makes it possible for us to find a home even in the dens of oppression, because "man must be at home somewhere before he can feel at home anywhere."[5]

Useni Eugene Perkins, the gifted author/poet, social practitioner, theorist, and social activist, in the tradition of our African-American living-dead ancestors/warriors dedicated his first major book to the harsh reality of contemporary life behind the wall. With a clear Black eye he confirms Dr. Thurman's insight in his seminal work, *Home Is A Dirty Street.*— He named this "dirty street" the ghetcolony in recognition of the fact that the place where most of us must now call home is not an isolated dynamic unique to the United States, but an internationally connected system, cousin to all of the underdeveloped colonies of the world. Unfortunately, those who are young, Black and oppressed in the U.S.A. must find a home within its confines or perish!

Home Is A Dirty Street addressed the first challenge of Blackness and the first act of liberation, i.e., it named the content and character of the "prison walls" with African eyes. As much as it affirmed our reality, it also raised significant questions like "what can be done to change and improve life for our youths who are young, Black, and entrapped and who should be instruments of the change." All questions raised by oppression dictate an answer from those who are oppressed.

Harvesting New Generations: The Positive Development of Black Youths is a brilliant, artist sequel to *Home Is A Dirty Street* that proffers answers for our future. It is a book of transcendency. It transcends naming the world of survival, and elevates us to a higher challenge of flourishing with sanity in the presence of our foe. With poignancy and grace, Useni tells us what must be done to transform our side of the line as well as dictate who must prepare the table of liberation for our children who are Black. Herein is the essence of *Harvesting New Generations*: finding and making a way for African-American youth to flourish with sanity intact, within and beyond the walls of the ghetcolony, not just as objects of history, but active subjects creating history and in the process, creating a new self and a new environment.

The Positive Development of Black Youth is no random path. Useni shows us that he knows that our children are the fruit of life, that a new fruitful harvest is inextricably connected to an organic balance of fertile soil and proper nourishment. In the human arena, optimum development emerges from the fertile soil of love, human solidarity, justice, and reason nourished by the presence of true freedom, activating stimuli, the absence of exploitative control and the presence of human centered modes of production. He acknowledges this truth. He also affirms that a people with no past has no future. Therefore, our future place must be our original starting place: Africa.

Africa is home, but it is no dirty street. It is the home of the original human being and the locality of the very first worldview. Useni returns to this original source for guidance, focus, and direction. He knows that "a people losing sight of origins are dead."[7] In this first chapter, "Legacy of Kunta Kente," he reminds us that the African slave trade disrupted the continuity of our human development and hurdled us into a hostile, life-taking, foreign environment, the ghetcolony, that made scapegoats of us, making us the criminals and the criminals' victims.

With razor sharp clarity and vitality, Useni dissects for us the tragedy, pitfalls, and imperatives of this travesty of oppression, declaring that without an African-centered education, consciousness, and conscience, replete with life enhancing values and institutions, we may continue to grow (expand), but we will not develop as a people, that is, we will not increase our skill capacity to be self-determinate and self-sufficient concomitantly nor will we control the dynamics of our destiny. If we refuse to start where we began, our new harvest will be ill-equipped to test all of our constructive possibilities as witnessed in chapter six (6), "Do Boys Bleed Too: The Crisis in Teenage Pregnancy." Only youths who are reintroduced to the fertile soil of the African way will develop the full capacity to destroy the historical walls that separate, alienate, and deprive us of our new human possibilities and at once be sufficiently skilled to erect a communal human monument that unifies African people and the world.

Useni's declaration of liberation is a prophesy for all of us who are destiny makers:

> ...all of the problems confronting Black people, and they are numerous and complex, the resolution of any one of them is inextricably linked to the quality of life we provide our young. It is irrational for a people to believe that their hopes and ambitions will ever be fully realized without developing their young...the ultimate survival of a people is largely dependent on the ability of their young to meet certain tasks, assume specific responsibilities and functions in the best interest of their race.

In his wisdom, Useni provides us with a conceptual guide and a meaningful role for us to sow the seed for a real Kwanza celebration.

Morris F.X. Jeff, Jr., DSW*

*Dr. Jeff, the director of the New Orleans City Welfare Department and the co-owner of the Counseling and Diagnostic Family Institute of New Orleans, Inc., is president of the National Association of Black Social Workers.

CHAPTER ONE

LEGACY OF KUNTA KENTE: THE EFFECTS OF SLAVERY ON BLACK YOUTH

> Thus, for Black Americans today
> the children of all the hundreds of
> Kunta Kentes unjustly chained
> in bondage—the early failure of
> this Nation's founders and their
> constitutional heirs to share the
> legacy of freedom with Black
> Americans is at least one factor in
> America's perpetual racial tensions.
>
> A. Leon Higginbotham, Jr.
> *In The Matter of Color, Race &*
> *The American Legal Process:*
> *The Colonial Period*

When the image of Kunta Kente, the unfailing hero of Alex Haley's highly acclaimed novel, *Roots*, caught the imagination of millions of readers, an episode in African American history was revealed that few people knew much about. In tracing his family roots to the small village of Juffure in Gambia, West Africa, Mr. Haley brought attention to the way African youths endured and coped with slavery after they were stolen from the motherland and taken through the perilous middle passage to the West Indies and then eventually to America.

The story of Kunta Kente became a legend within months after the publication of *Roots*, and millions of readers and viewers of the television adaptation of the book were either stunned or awed by the accounts of his experiences. They were provided with glimpses into the life of an African boy who had undergone a traumatic cultural and social transformation — despite his stubbornness to hold on to his own African heritage.

From the day young Kunta Kente was captured and forced into bondage, his life became disoriented, paradoxical, and severely stressful. His early childhood in Juffure was of particular interest because it described the orderly process of maturation that was so akin to most African societies. Indeed, Kunta Kente was the product of a society that held its young in high esteem and developed a network of role models and functional institutions to assist him in his social development. Until the day he was attacked and kidnapped by slavers, Kunta Kente had been raised in a fashion that clearly defined who he was, his responsibility to his parents, relatives, and community, and his sense of manhood. The latter revelation was learned during the Poro (rites of passage) that prepared young males for their adult lives. The "rites of passage" was perhaps the most important stage in an African boy's life, for it not only indoctrinated him with the spiritual and cultural manifestations of his people's traditions, but was the catalyst that consummated his manhood. African girls participated in a similar type of training during their puberty which prepared them for womanhood. Womanhood carried with it great importance in African societies and each society helped to prepare a girl for this important role.

In contemporary Black America, the only ceremony that

approximates the African youth's "rites of passage" may be the coronation which introduces young men and women to Black middle class society. However, this is primarily an elitest affair that focuses on social status rather than social development. Kunta Kente's childhood was filled with the excitement and exuberance that were common to most African children. Despite the famine that nearly devastated his village and the other hardships endured by a people whose survival is dependent upon the resources of the earth, his childhood experiences were rewarding and beneficial. Ingrained in the social intrastructure of Juffure, regardless of how parochial it may appear, there existed a systematic pattern of developing children which is the antithesis of what takes place in our present day Black communities that are wedged in the racist armour of white America.

Although the story of Kunta Kente may not be typical of all African youths, or for that matter constitute an actual documentation, it does provide us with some knowledge of the social and cultural systems which shaped their lives. While there exist a multiplicity of African cultures with diversities among them, almost all African communities have developed socialization systems to enhance the lives of their members. In his studies of African cultures, Edward Wilmot Blyden summarizes this phenomenon: "The African has developed and organized a system useful to him for all the needs of life."[1]

Another description of this orderly system of socializing African children can be seen in the following statement about the rearing of children in Acholi, Uganda in East Africa:

> African People take great care to see that children are given all the necessary training in order that they will be hard-working and useful men and women in the society . . . Great attention is paid to all aspects of children's "moral" development.[2]

In particular, the family and its extended relationships played an important role in the rearing of African youths. The African youth was the center of family life and his socialization became the shared responsibility of all family members:

African children grow up in an intense situation of kinship and family. They continue throughout their lives to learn their family obligations and family histories. And, perhaps most importantly, they learn from a very early age to spread their regard, their rewards and their concern.³

Thus, the African youth was highly disciplined and respectful toward his family and elders. His childhood and pre-adolescent experiences were arranged in an orderly fashion that helped him to adapt to the values and morals of his society. As a result, the African youth seldom violated the sanctions and customs of his community. Quite the contrary, the African youth became an example of his culture as well as the conveyor of its values.

But the advent of the slave trade, started by Portugal in the early 1500's, and later intensified by Spain and England around 1562, after Sir John Hawkins' exploratory voyage to Africa, disrupted this orderly process for millions of African youths. As in the story of Kunta Kente, African youth were uprooted from their communities and became the assailable targets of this dehumanizing enterprise which in the late 1760's sent countless millions across the turbulent Atlantic Ocean, the hub of the Middle Passage. Youths were a high priority among slavers because it was felt they could be more easily controlled for the slave market. An account by one slaver identifies his human cargo:

> The cargo consisted of a hundred and thirty slaves of whom two-thirds were males and one-third females. The two sexes were kept separate by a partition or bulk-head, built from side to side, across the ship, alloting the waist to the men and to the women, the quarter deck. A great majority of them were very young, being from ten to eighteen years of age.⁴

Once an African youth was placed into bondage and seasoned at one of the islands in the West Indies, he then became a subject of the institution of slavery. Though many slave youths remained on the islands, i.e., Jamaica, Haiti, Cuba, the emphasis in this commentary is confined to those who lived in North America. No doubt a commentary on slave youths raised in the West Indies would possibly explain why there are distinct differences in behavior between Black American youths from the aforementioned countries. For example, during my brief visits to Haiti and Jamaica, I found little evidence of serious juvenile crime despite the fact these two countries are among the poorest and possibly most oppressed in the West Indies. One reason for this could be due to these countries' punitive laws which have no tolerance for delinquent behavior. Still another reason could be because the slaves who remained in the West Indies were able to retain vestiges of their African culture which placed high value on discipline and obedience among its young. If the latter is true, it deserves further study to ascertain its revelancy to Black youth in America. However, we can, with unequivocal authority, assume that regardless of the types of slave systems employed in other countries, slavery was a dehumanizing institution which left indelible scars on those it enslaved.

And so it was this disengagement of family, home and culture that made Kunta Kente's new experience as a slave not only frightful but one filled with painful nostalgia:

> Would he ever grow up to be a man like Omoro? He wondered if his father still thought of him; and if his mother had given to Lamen, Suwadu, and Madi the love that had been taken away from her when he was stolen. He thought of all of Juffure, and of how he had never realized more than now how very deeply he loved his village.[5]

Having been stolen from his motherland; endured the excruciating voyage of the Middle Passage; beaten by a toubab for trying to maintain his true identity; Kunta Kente, at the young age of seventeen, had undergone a profound social and cultural metamorphosis. The values he had learned as a child in Juffure and the strong kinship bond he had with members of his community were now becoming blurred memories, fading with each crimson sunset. After living his childhood and pre-adolescent years in the unperturbed security of his native land, Kunta Kente was now destined to live the remainder of his life in a foreign and hostile environment. And it was within this antagonistic environment that Kunta Kente and millions like him continued their socialization; but now under an oppressive system which showed no concern for their welfare. In Juffure, Kunta Kente had been groomed to become a man in conpliance with the values of his society; now he would be deprogrammed to be a chattel in compliance with the racist statues of American slavery.

Despite the massive volumes of literature written about slavery, there have been few books that have seriously dealt with how this oppressive system affected Black youths. On the contrary, the literature on slavery has mostly been centered on the affects of slavery on adults and the impact it has had in shaping the Black Experience in America. Even though Black youths have been an integral part of the Black Experience, the literature has relegated them to an insignificant status. Yet we cannot fully appreciate the social and cultural dynamics of the Black Experience until we view it from a developmental continuum; that is, to see the Black adult as an extension of his childhood experiences. Although the literature on slavery has rendered a disservice to Black youths, it is possible to extrapolate from this literature threads of information about how they lived under slavery. Regardless of the die-hard racists who even today try to justify American slavery as being an economic necessity to save the south, the evidence we are privy to is overwhelmingly opposed to this argument. Also, the rationale espoused by some apologists of slavery that it embraced Christian principles because it allegedly tried to make converts out of pagans is equally insidious. The fact remains that American slavery violated the human dignity of man, and subjected a race of people to the most degrading, oppressive system in the annals of human history. The imminent historian Lerone Bennett, Jr. makes the following remarks about American's "peculiar institution":

> For two hundred years, black, brown and yellow men and women were held in bondage in America. During two hundred years, "a social system as coercive as any yet known" was erected on the flimsy framework of "the most implacable race-consciousness yet observed in virtually

any society"...Behind this Cotton Curtain, four million human beings were systematically deprived of every right of personality. Vice, immorality, and brutality were institutionalized.[6]

John Hope Franklin, another distinguished historian, collaborates Mr. Bennett's statement.

The brutality which apparently was inherent in a system of human exploitation existed in every community where slavery was established. The wastefulness and extravagance of the plantation system made no exception of human resources. Slaves were for economic gain, and if beating them would increase their efficiency, and this was generally believed, then, the rod and lash should not be spared.[7]

It was within this type of dehumanizing environment that Black youths had to learn to survive. No longer could they rely upon the organized social systems which were typical of their native communities. The slave plantation bore no resemblance to their native communities and was, in fact, inimical to everything they embraced. The mark of bondage was branded on their not yet fully developed bodies, and a new type of African youth was being molded out of the oppressive fabric of American slavery. First, the new African youth was stripped of his African name and given an English one instead. (Note the resistence of Kunta Kente to accept the name Toby, given him by his slavemaster.) The changing of the African youth's original name was one way the slavemaster attempted to destroy his native language and to isolate him from members of his same community and from those whose language bore some similarity. The African youth who was born in his mother country and brought to America as a slave was almost always separated from his family. Thus separation usually took place in his mother country, before the Middle Passage and seasoning in the West Indies. Most of these youths were between the ages of 8 and 10, although there are accounts of younger aged children who were taken into captivity. These children received little guidance and were left pretty much on their own until they were old enough to keep up with the older youths. Youths ten and over were considered to be adults and, therefore, assumed the occupational functions assigned to the women and men.

Those children born into slavery, that is, who were the offsprings of a slave woman were automatically assigned to the mother, regardless of who the father was. Many slave states enacted legislature to ensure that this policy would be legally recognized. Of course the primary motive for this arrangement was to guarantee that a child given birth by a slave, even if the woman had a miscegenationist relationship, would automatically be a slave at birth.

> It was, therefore, significant from an economic standpoint whether a child derived its status from its mother or its father. Once it was established that the Black woman's child took the mother's status, the master does gain a crucial economic advantage—its labor force reproduced itself.[8]

Often the slavemaster's efforts to control the lives of the slave children born by his women slaves were outrageously conceived, as described in the following two examples.

> For instance, in a 1646 contract, Frances Potts sold a Black woman and child to Stephen Carlton, "to use forever." Another deed records William Whittington's sale of a girl merely ten years old; looking to the future he noted that she was sold along with any issue (children) she might produce for her and her children's "lifetime" and their successors forever."[9]

Much has been written about slavery's adverse effect on the family, especially the separation of slave children from their fathers and the lack of "parenting" from their mothers. In my research, I found the former to be true most of the time, although some slaveowners realized the importance of family stability and encouraged fathers to live with their families. This was particularly true of the small plantation owner who had to maximize the collective labor of his slaves to maintain his own economic stability. But even under this system, the father had little influence over his offsprings and was detached from their normal experiences. Conversely, owners of large plantations almost always kept the men, father included, in special quarters. However, there were also many examples of families sharing a common household on both types of plantations. But as Lerone Bennett aptly states, "Fatherhood, under this system, was a monstrous joke; fatherhood, in fact, was virtually abolished."[10]

In regard to the mother's role in rearing her children, it, too, was reduced to just a few motherly chores. Indeed, the slave mother had few opportunities to care for her children. Instead, to quote Lerone Bennett again:

> Slave women, for example usually had little or nothing to do with the raising of their children. They went to the fields in the mornings and left their children at plantation nurseries.[11]

Even though the slave mother spent little time with her children, LaFrances Rodgers-Rose feels that slavery did not destroy the intimate relationship which normally exists between a mother and her child.

> What I am suggesting is that the bond that existed between mother and child in African society continued in slavery; although the structure of that relationship had changed; the crucial process of care, love, and devotion continued.[12]

Ms. Rodger-Rose's analysis may be true of first generation slave mothers, who had experienced the "socialization" of African motherhood, but this would be difficult under a system that kept the mother away from her children. However, few of us would deny the fact slave mothers longed to love and care for their children. There exist too numerous accounts of slave mothers who took extraordinary measures to preserve their families. Still it is apparent that slavery did change the pattern of family life which had been cultivated in African society. But the evidence, when closely examined, does not support the thesis it was completely aborted. As we should discern in other chapters, the Black family has been the nexus for maintaining our survival.

Black youths became the central nerve of the slave institution. Since slavery consisted of not only physical bondage but mental bondage as well, the slavemaster knew this system could survive only to the extent it was able to perpetuate itself. Therefore the adolescent years became crucial, for a rebellious youth, embued with contempt for his slavemaster, would never become a good, obedient slave. If the slavemaster could control the minds of his young slaves, to become more resigned toward slavery and fearful of him, incidences of escapes and even insurrections would be greatly minimized. The older a slave became, the least his slavemaster had to worry about the slave retaliating against him. However, most older slaves were held in high reverence by the young who seldom challenged their wisdom. This is not to suggest that older slaves were not threats to their slavemasters. The lives of slaves such as Harriet Tubman, Frederick Douglass, and Nat Turner would invalidate this flawed reasoning. But the point being made here is that the adolescent years were pivotal to the manner in which a slave viewed himself, his slavemaster, and his future adult life. Vyry, the heroine of Margaret Walker's prize winning novel, *Jubilee*, first begins to think seriously about her freedom when she was fifteen. After developing an infatuation for a free black named Randall Ware, who approaches her for marriage, she begins to contemplate what it would be like to be free.

> She had never before entertained the faintest idea or hope of freedom, except some dream of an answer to prayers, when God would suddenly appear and send a deliverer like Moses, and set free all the people who were in bondage such as she ... Now the idea of being free began to take hold of her and to work up and down and through her like milk churning to make butter.[13]

Once a slave got the impulse for freedom, the chances of him/her being an obedient slave were significantly lowered. And the earlier this impulse came in the life of a slave, the more difficult he was to reckon with as an adult. To counter this tendency, slavemasters did everything possible to distill from the minds of their young slaves a longing for freedom. This is one of the principal reasons slavemasters were leery of the younger slaves congregating with older slaves. Although the older slaves may have been obedient toward their slavemaster, they harbored much resentment and hostility which the slavemaster did not want transferred to the young. In his exhaustive and scholarly study of Black family life from 1750-1925, Herbert G. Gutman cites the diary of one slavemaster who tried to maintain discipline over his young slaves:

> "A serious obstacle to that discipline, Barrow's records reveal, was what younger slaves learned from older slaves."[14]

About one of his older slaves named Big Lucy, Barrow said, "(She) corrupts every young Negro in her power."[15] Mr. Gutman summarizes Barrow's dilemma: "Far too many young slaves listened to Big Lucy, and her message was not one that Barrow wanted them to hear."[16]

To maintain and to perpetuate the plantation system it was important for the slavemaster to buffer his young slaves' thirst for freedom. Simply to resell those slaves who were not responsive to his demands, and buy new ones, was generally not economically practical. And capital gain was the slavemaster's main concern regardless of how ruthless he had to be to ensure his plantation system prospered and survived.

We can get another glimpse into the slave experiences of Black youths from the various slave narratives which were written either by the slaves, themselves, or in most cases with the assistance of a white co-author. Although the latter narratives may be suspect, and serve the interest of the white co-author, we should try to be objective in our appraisal of them. The most celebrated slave narrative, published in 1789, (which had an 8th printing by 1794) *The Life of Olaudahh Equiano or Gustavus Vassa the African*, was an amazing and detailed account of Gustavus Vassa's childhood in Benin, West Africa before captivity, during slavery, and as a free man. In many ways his recollections of his initiation into slavery are similar to Kunta Kente's experiences.

I now saw myself deprived of all chances of returning to my native country, or even the least glimpse of hope of gaining the share, which I now considered as friendly; and I even wished for my former slavery in preference to my present situation, which was filled with horrors of every kind, still heightened by my ignorance of what I was to undergo.[17]

Upon his arrival in America, Gustavus Vassa was placed on a plantation in Virginia and, again, like Kunta Kente found few people he could communicate with.

I was a few weeks weeding grass and gathering stones in a plantation; and at least all my companions (other slaves) were distributed different, and only myself was left. I was now exceedingly miserable, and thought myself worst off than any of the rest of my companions, for they could talk to each other, but I had no person to speak to that I could understand.[18]

In his slave narrative, James W.C. Pennington, a blacksmith, made this emotional statement about his childhood:

To estimate the sad state of a slave child, you must look at it as a helpless human being thrown upon the world without the benefit of its natural guardians. It is thrown into the world without a social circle to flee to for hope, shelter, comfort, or instruction. The social circle, with all its heaven-ordained blessings, is of the utmost importance to the tender child (free child); but of this, the slave child, however, tender and delicate, is robbed.[19]

Another view of childhood is provided by Frederick Douglass in the first of his three narratives.

The slaveholder, having nothing to fear from impotent childhood, easily afford to refrain from cruel inflections; and if cold and hunger do not pierce the tender frame, the first seven or eight years of the slave-boy's life are about as full of sweet content as those of the most favored and petted white children of the slaveholder.[20]

However, Frederick Douglass' perception of slavery changed dramatically when he was 16 years old and purchased by Mr. Covey, the "Negro Breaker."

> I shall never be able to narrate half the mental experience through which it was my lot to pass, during my stay at Covey's. I was completely wrecked, changed, and bewildered, goaded almost to madness at one time, and at another reconciling myself to my wretched condition.[21]

The narrative of another famous Black spokesman, Booker T. Washington, provides some revealing insights into his early life as a slave.

> One of my earliest recollections is that of my mother cooking a chicken late at night, and awakening the children for the purpose of feeding them. How or where she got it, I do not know. I presume, however, it was procured from our owner's farm. Some people may call this theft. If such a thing was to happen now, I should condemn it as theft myself. But taking place at the time it did, and for the reason that it did, no one could ever make me believe that my mother was guilty of thieving. She was simply a victim of the system of slavery.[22]

Obviously as a product of the same oppressive system, Booker T. Washington felt no shame in what his mother had done. About his chores on the plantation, he says:

> During the period that I spent in slavery, I was not large enough to be of much service, still I was occupied most of the time in cleaning the yards, carrying water to men in the fields or going to the mill to which I used to take corn once a week, to be ground.[23]

Yet his most frustrating experience was recorded as follows:

> The most trying ordeal that I was forced to endure as a slave boy, however, was the wearing of a flax shirt. In the part of Virginia where I lived it was common to use flax as a part of the clothing for slaves. That part of the flax from which clothing was made was largely the refuse, which of course was the cheapest and roughest part. I can scarcely imagine any torture, except, perhaps, the pulling of a tooth that is equal to that caused by putting on a new flax shirt for the first time.[24]

And in the same narrative, Booker T. Washington provides us with his philosophical view of Black Youth.

The world should not pass judgement upon the Negro, and especially upon the Negro youth, too quickly or too harshly. The Negro boy has obstacles, discouragements, and temptations to battle with that are little known to those not situated as he is. When a white boy undertakes a task, it is taken for granted that he will succeed. On the other hand, people are usually surprised if the Negro boy does not fail. In a word, the Negro youth starts out with the presumption against him.[25]

As one might expect, there is even less material on the early lives of African slave women. Erlene Stetson provides the following explanation for this unfortunate situation.

... scholars treat the slavery experience as a Black male phenomenon, regarding Black women as biological functionaries whose destines are rendered ephemeral—to lay their eggs and die. Thus, predictably, the tales of slave rebellions (not merely slave resistance) offer masculine images of active dynamic personages—fighting—excluding almost entirely women who actively resisted and rebelled, though not always by escaping ... Only the near mythicized sagas of Harriet Tubman and Sojourner Truth have escaped obscurity.[26]

Since slave narratives are the most accessible source for looking at slave experiences of Black youths, we are compelled to extract from this source most of our information about Black female slaves. It should also be noted, however, that slave narratives by Black women have a higher ratio of white co-authors than those by Black men.

In one slave narrative by Linda Brent, we learn of a slave girl's ambivalence about slavery when her mistress dies. Her first sentiments are highly emotional and sympathetic.

When I was nearly twelve years old, my kind mistress sickened and died. As I saw the cheek grow paler, and the eye more glassy, how earnestly I prayed in my heart that she might live! I loved her; for she had been almost like a mother to me.[27]

In another passage, however, Linda Brent changes her sympathetic attitudes toward her (dead mistress) when she is informed she is not set free when her mistress's will is read.

> After a brief period of suspense, the will of my mistress was read, and we learned that she had bequeathed me to her sister's daughter, a child of five year old.[28]

Linda Brent realizes, then, the real meaning of slavery, and how discompassionate slave owners actually were, regardless of their professed benevolency: "These God-breathing machines are no more, in the sight of their masters, than the cotton they plant, or the horses they tend."[29]

She continues to abhor slavery when she describes the ordeals she encounters as an adolescent.

> But I now entered on my fifteenth year—a sad epoch in the life of a slave girl. My master began to whisper foul words in my ear. Young as I was, I could not remain ignorant of their import... He peopled my young mind with unclean images, such as only a vile monster could think of.[30]

The "vile monster" was Dr. Flint, her new slave master who was determined to sexually exploit her.

> No pen can give an adequate description of the all pervading corruption produced by slavery. The slave girl is reared in an atmosphere of licentiousness and fear.[31]

Finally at the age of 21, after mothering a baby girl, Linda Brent escapes to the north, and begins to fervently speak out against the inhumane system that had wrecked most of her young life. Only the memory of her grandmother provides her with the strength to endure the future.

> It has been painful to me, in many ways, to recall the dreary years I passed in bondage. I would gladly forget them if I could. Yet, the retrospection is not altogether without solace; for with those gloomy recollections come tender memories of my good old grandmother, like light, fleecy clouds floating over a dark and troubled sea.[32]

Of course these few and abbreviated examples do not

provide us with a comprehensive description of slavery's impact on Black youths. I would suggest for the reader who is engrossed by this subject to read the full documents from which I have quoted. Despite the fragmentary information presented here, I do feel some valid conclusions can be made.

1. While there still exist considerable debate over whether or not slavery destroyed the principle socializing elements of African societies, it is reasonable to assume that most of these elements were damaged, leaving Black youths with few traditional models to enhance their social development.

2. Black youths were forced to develop their own coping skills because of the fragmentation of the family unit and the systematic suppression of parental and adult influence.

3. Black youths were groomed for manual labor and denied any educational training which would allow them to compete competitively in a western dominated culture.

4. Black youths were rarely disciplined for misconduct or violence confined to their own group, but were severely punished when they violated sanctions which fostered the institution of slavery.

5. Black youths were reseasoned to function as obedient and loyal servents and relegated to a status of human chattel without any legal protection for their welfare.

6. Black girls were sexually exploited at will by any white male, and treated as though they were merely concubines. Simply, their most important function was that of breeding children.

7. Black boys were denied their traditional manhood and encouraged to become sexual gluttons to father children for economic convenience.

8. Black youths were taught to inhibit their true emotion so they would appear to be one dimensional, predictable, and lacking in human feelings.

9. Black youths' transition to adulthood was marred by the absence of any formal recognition to establish their social status, social roles, and social responsibilities.

10. Black youths constituted an oppressed minority within a larger oppressed minority, possessing no rights to arbitrate their destinies.

The aforementioned conclusions may also, to some degree, be attributed to the status of adult slaves. But this commentary is primarily concerned with the social development of Black youths. And, obviously, the manner in which they developed became the foundation upon which their adulthood was built. Likewise, the manner in which our contemporary Black youths develop will serve as the foundation for tomorrow's adults.

The evolution of human development must be viewed from its generic base, for the formation of a people's fundamental being (existence) is not cultivated in years, but centuries and even eons. This view is derived from the science of culturology which is summarized as follows:

> Since the earliest days of human history every member of the human species has been introduced at birth into a cultural environment of beliefs, customs, instruments, expressions of art, et., as well as a natural habital of climate, topography, slora, and sauna. This cultural environment is a continuum, a tradition; it descends lineally from one generation to another, and it may diffuse laterally from one people to another.[33]

A more detailed discussion of this science will be discussed in the next chapter, for it contains, I believe, an inestimable amount of knowledge to help us better understand the plural or multi-cultural structure of American society in which we live. The legend of Kunta Kente and the thousands of other African youths, therefore, becomes the evolutionary base from which we will continue to evaluate and explore the social and cultural experiences of today's Black youths. For if we are concerned about their destiny, and it is imperative that we are, we must construct new directions, new institutions, and new values to salvage their lives so we can survive and prosper as a people, a race, a nation.

It was necessary in this commentary to begin with the effects of slavery on Black youths to construct a frame of reference for understanding the behavior of contemporary Black youths. This introspection enables us to identify those values, both negative and positive, which Black youth embraced in coping with slavery. These values need to be taken into consideration if we are serious about the development of today's Black youth. Despite the adverse influence of slavery, Black youth must have developed certain strengths which were necessary for their survival; thus the survival of Black people. The fact that Black youths were able to survive under the institution of slavery is an achievement we too often overlook. In my work with Black youths, over twenty five years, I have found that many adults are so completely oblivious to these strengths. Instead, they look at the vast majority of Black youths as social deviants who have contributed little to our survival. Yet Black youths must be given some credit for the few gains we have made. This acknowledgement is based upon the fact that the adolescent years are pivotal to the development of a people. This is the period when values and attitudes are solidified which later become fixed during the adult years. I'm aware that many practitioners of human development claim the formative years as having the greatest impact on personality. No doubt there is truth in this, but regardless of the mold that shapes behavior during the formative years, this should not mean it is irreversible. To merely accept the postulation that behavior is inflexible after childhood provides us with little incentive to improve the lives of adolescents. But I have known many adolescents, whose formative years left much to be desired, overcome their problems and become positive adult models. Conversely, I have known adolescents whose formative years were very positive become negative adult models. These examples suggest that the adolescent years often become the prevailing factor in shaping adult behavior. And it is during adolescence that most Black youths encounter the full impact of racism that tend to destroy any chance they have to become positive adult models. This is the period when a disporportionate number of Black youth become entrenched in the Juvenile Justice System, exhibit self-defeating behavior, become hooked on drugs, drop out of school, show disrespect of their elders, rebel against authority, and display mannerisms that are often repugnant and repulsive. Thus, the adolescent years are most critical in the development process that culminates into adulthood.

However, the behavior of Black youth has not always been characterized by negative attitudes as attested by the strengths that helped many to overcome and cope with seemingly insurmountable obstacles to become productive adults in our struggle for freedom. Had they not possessed these strengths, our situation, today, would be compounded by even greater injustices. What, then, are some of the strengths which enabled Black youth, under slavery, to survive and maintain a level of behavior that has contributed to our development as a people? Some of these strengths can be identified as:

1. The ability to adapt to an oppressive environment without being totally debilitated by it.

2. The ability to survive with little guidance from formal institutions and a cohesive family structure.

3. The strong desire to be free.

4. A strong work orientation that allowed them to assume adult responsibilities.

5. A high regard and respect for elders.

6. An obedient attitude that was necessary if slaves were to function in a cooperative manner for the general welfare of all.

These strengths, and undoubtedly many more, were necessary to survive slavery. Unfortunately, over the years, many of them have deteriorated. As a result, some Black youths have developed a different set of attitudes which do not always serve the best interest of the Black community. What happened to these strengths? Can any of them be revived? These are questions we must ask ourselves if we are truly concerned with the positive development of Black youth. The more salient challenge is how to institutionalize these strengths so that they will become an appendage of our ethos. This is the task we have before us, to rejuvenate those strengths which are anchored in the struggles of any oppressed people. This is the harvest we must sow for future generations.

SOCIALIZATION ENVIRONMENT OF BLACK YOUTH
(African Roots to Present)

	Environmental Characteristics	Behavior Outcomes
AFRICAN ROOTS	- supportive environment - stable family unit - close kinship bonds - supportive institutions - well-defined roles - Rites of Passage	- highly discipline - positive self-concept - prosocial - cultural competence - self-appreciation
CAPTIVITY AND MIDDLE PASSAGE	- death (90-100 million) - uprooted kinship bonds - physical punishment	- suppressed behavior - psychological scars - damaged self-concept
AMERICAN SLAVERY	- suppression of culture - hostile environment - suppression of family - distortion of images - disruption of Rites of Passage	- suppressed behavior - adaptive behavior - self-diffusion - cultural incompetence - confused self-concept - psychological scars - depreciated character
SO-CALLED EMANCIPATION	- hostile environment - institutional racism - colonized education - suppression of family - colonized culture - scientific colonialism	- adaptive behavior - dependent behavior - cultural incompetence - suppressed behavior - psychological scars - self-diffusion - confused self-concept
POST-RECONSTRUCTION TO PRESENT	- hostile environment - scientific colonialsim - institutional racism - colonized education - colonized culture - ghetcolony - street institution	- adaptive behavior - depreciated character - cultural incompetence - psychological scars - ambivalent behavior - self-diffusion - reactionary behavior - confused self-concept

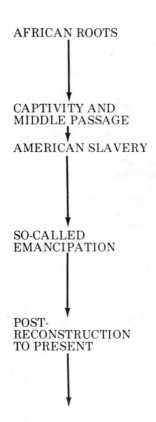

Useni

CHAPTER TWO

BLAME ME ON MY CULTURE
THE VICTIM AS SCAPEGOAT

> A people losing sight of origins are
> dead. A people deaf to purposes
> are lost. Under fertile rain, in
> scorching sunshine there is no
> difference: their bodies are mere
> corpses, awaiting final burial.
>
> Ayi Kwei Armah
> *Two Thousand Seasons*

Ralph Armstrong, age 19, had just left the warehouse shaped building that houses the unemployment office on Chicago's west side. His departure was abrupt and unruly as though he had been "turned off" by someone. As he began to walk toward Ogden Avenue, his thick black fingers holding an unlit cigarette, he tried to buffer his pent up emotions with a swaggering strut that typified his version of masculine toughness. When he approached the intersection, he was warmly greeted by a friend who immediately responded with the ritual of slapping hands.

"Hey man, what it is?"

Ralph pretended to be unnerved by the gesture.

"Same ole shit. Ain't nothing changed." "Look like you have my man," replied his friend in a tone of concern.

"Like I told you ain't nothin' changed."

"If dats the case, why you lookin so down?"

"Cause dats the way I feel."

"And how's dat?"

"Why you askin' so many questions?"

"I'm your friend, baby. I dig you. So why don't you run it down to me, you dig?"

Sensing his friend was really concerned, Ralph lights his cigarette and takes a deep inhale.

"Well, it ain't dat much to talk about. I just left the unemployment office to check out a gig, you dig? I waited almost three hours before I was interviewed."

"Is dat all," his friend retorted. "Why the last time I was dere, I din't get a chance to see nobody."

Unimpressed by his friend's remark, Ralph takes the last puff from his cigarette and then flicks it on the ground.

"Anyway, they had this gig you dig, workin' in one of dose mail order houses. Didn't pay much, but tight as things are, I didn't give a damn."

"I can dig it."

"So when I filled out the application, the lady looked at it."

"And?"

"She said I wasn't qualified cause I din't have a high school diploma. Can you imagine—a high school diploma just to put some fuckin' boxes on the shelves!

"What you expect, my man. You got to be able to read what's on the boxes." He begins to snicker.

"Ain't nothin' funny."

"Sorry, man."

"I can read enough to do dat!"

"Can you really, man. I mean when we were in school—you din't do much action."

"I had other things on my mind. And anyway, you know after I got busted, I din't learn a damn thing at St. Charles." (St. Charles is a reform school.)

"Whose fault was that?"

"Mine, I suppose."

"You suppose. Man you know if you don't have education together, you ain't shit!"

"Yeah, I suppose you right. I really blew it din't I?"

The two young men stare at each other and after a few moments of silence, Ralph reaches for two cigarettes, gives one to his friend and then lights his own. They then proceed to cross the street, Ralph resuming his masculine strut as if to compensate for something he never had.

The scene that has been described is not uncommon in the Black community. Young Black males like Ralph and his friend comprise a large population who are unable to find work, and most likely will never hold a permanent job. While there exist many reasons that contribute to their problems, many believe they are their own "worst enemy" because of their failure to become employable. This failure has made them the subjects of considerable "social labeling" which has attempted to define their economic plight. In a report financed by the Ford Foundation, this dismal situation was described as follows:

The approach to the labor market significantly dichotomizes the respective positions of ghetto (Black) and of the middle class youths. In this arena the Black youth's deprivation—in regard to education, race, social class, lack of proper role models—severely handicaps him or her.[1]

This is even more true today in view of the severe economic depression that grips the country. While unemployment has always been high for Black youths—today the figures are staggering, as high as 60% in some urban communities. However, today's unemployed Black youth are no longer identified as just being "chronic unemployed" or "unskilled." Now they are being labeled by society's most recent sociological lexicon, "the underclass." Although this is not a new term, in many ways it approximates the socialist classification of the lumpen-proletarian, it has now become a convenient and fashionable term to define a population, mostly young Blacks, ages 17-25, who are aliens to the job market.

In 1982, the situation had become so grim that it became the subject of a Times Magazine cover story.

The barricades are seen only fleetingly by most middle class Americans as they rush by in their cars or commuter trains . . . But out there is a different world, a place of pock-marked streets, gutted tenements and broken hopes . . . Behind its crumbling walls lives a large group of people who are more intractable, more socially alien and more hostile than almost anything imagined. They are the unreachables: the American Underclass.[2]

This latent discovery by Times Magazine only reveals the "time lag" that exist between social reality and the media. If the publishers of this nationally recognized journal had searched earlier it would've known that the so-called "underclass" is not a new phenomenon, but a way of life many Blacks have lived for years. Its existence is predictable because its genesis has been nurtured by economic exploitation, political suppression and racial oppression. Douglas G. Glasgow, the author of *The Black Underclass* supports this prediction.

Racism is probably the most basic cause of the underclass condition. Racism in the sixties was different. The "for colored" and "whites only" signs of the thirties and forties had been removed, but the institutions of the country were more completely saturated with covert expressions of racism than ever."[3]

In his book, Glasgow describes his study of Black youth who participated in the revolt in Watts, California which set off a chain reaction in other depressed Black communities across the country. Glasgow's findings revealed that most of these youths have not progressed from the social despair which ignited their emotions in 1965.

The young fire brands of Watts were (and nearly all still are) part of what has recently been dubbed the underclass, a group whose emergence as a permanent fixture of our nation's social structure represents one of the most significant class developments in the past two decades.[4]

Predictably, like so many other sociological terms that have tried to articulate the status of Black youth entangled in a web of racism and oppression, the word "underclass" becomes not only a stigma but a badge. And it is a badge the wearer earns not for his heroic deeds, but for his alledged misdeeds. Simply he is a member of this infamous group because he has failed to make use of the resources society provides for him. Instead he is held responsible for his failure because he "blew" the opportunities offered to him by society. Indeed, he becomes the scapegoat who now must survive the best he can, for society's resources have done the best they could.

Although Ralph's situation may be a crude example of how the victim, due to his own frustrations and inabilities to solve his problem, turns inwardly and accepts the blame that he is in fact the problem. It is a rationale espoused by many.

"They just won't learn."

"Some of them don't give a damn!"

"If only they didn't come from broken homes, maybe they'd have a chance."

"There must be something wrong with them."

"What do you expect? Look at their neighborhoods."

In one of his nationally televised speeches, President Reagan, after perusing through the ads of the New York Times, commented that there simply existed a shortage of skilled people to fill positions. Implicit in his remarks was the failure of the unemployed to take advantage of the job opportunities which were available. Of course these jobs existed primarily in the fields of medicine, engineering, computer science, and other highly technological professions, occupations few Blacks have had the opportunity to pursue. President Reagan's caustic comments did not take this into consideration but, instead, gave the impression that the unemployed were out of work because they lacked self motivation. To be sure, some rationale had to be conjured to explain why so many Blacks are unable to "mainstream" into the affluent job market.

Blaming the victim has become an academic diatribe to explain the reasons Black people have not taken full advantage of the so-called American dream. It distorts cause and effect relationships to make the victim appear to be the culprit for the problem that consumes him. Even though the diatribe does not always blame the victim per se, it obstensibly raises questions about the quality of the victim's culture. The aforementioned Time Magazine article also cites:

> Though its members come from all races and live in many places, the underclass is made up mostly of impoverished urban Blacks, who still suffer from the heritage of slavery and discrimination.[5]

Obviously, the cogent words in this benign statement are "still suffer from the heritage of slavery and discrimination." At first glance this statement may appear to be sympathetic to the condition of Blacks; however, a critical examination of it reveals that it actually blames the victim's culture (heritage) for inducing the problem in which the victim finds himself. Since the individual is the product of his culture, it is necessary to malign his culture to make him feel a sense of guilt or shame. For if he is the product of a deprived, disadvantaged and pathological culture, he must automatically assume its characteristics. And, in this identity formation, the victim can sometimes feel relieved, because whatever are his self-perceived faults, he can blame them on his culture. As a result, the victim, because he identifies with his culture, does not always understand the actual reasons why he is being victimized. Consequently, the victim becomes endoctrinated with self-defeating attitudes which stifle his development. And, regardless of the evidence that may be contrary to his self-perception, the victim is unable to overcome the stigmas associated with his culture. By depreciating the victim's culture, it becomes easier to shift the blame from the institutions which are supposed to assist in his socialization.

There continues to exist a significant number of scholars, many Blacks included, who persist in labeling the culture of Black people as "culturally deprived, culturally disadvantaged, etc." These terms became popular during the sixties and can be attributed, in part, to Frank Reissman's widely acclaimed, *The Culturally Deprived Child.* Though Reissman claims his intentions were sincere and based on his experiences with Black "underpriviledged children," these terms produced a "cult" of supposedly well-intentioned scholars who were dismayed by the low achievement scores of many Black children. This academic diatribe was particularly prevalent in the field of education as evidenced by the following statement which attempted to explain the so-called cognitive deficiencies in Black children.

> The consequence of cognitive deficiencies in culturally deprived children (Black children) are complicated by their pattern of motivation and attitudes. Psychologist describe the characteristic syndrome of feelings and attitudes of the cultural deviates as follows: such children have a feeling of alienation induced by family climate and experience combined with a debilitatingly low self-concept; they tend to question their own worth, to fear being challenged, and to exhibit a desire to cling to the familiar; they have many feelings of guilt and shame. These children are wary: their trust in adults is limited; they make trigger like responses and are hyperactive; they are quick to vent hostility orally and physically. In other ways they are apathetic, unresponsive and lack initiative. It is difficult for them to form meaningful relationships.[6]

This statement, taken from a thesis manufactured by two nationally influential educators, is so loaded with academic diatribe, i.e., alienation, debilitatingly, low self-concept, hyperactive, hostility, apathetic, unresponsive, cultural deviant, etc., one would think it was a discussion about untamed animals. As one can readily discern, these definitions only give credance to the "blaming the victim" syndrome. But what makes this syndrome so deceptive is the veil that hides its true motive.

Victim-blaming is cloaked in kindness and concern, and bears all the trappings and statistical furbelows of science: it is obscured by a perfumed haze of humanitarianism.[7]

Samuel F. Yette, a former *Newsweek* correspondent, provides his analysis of this manipulant practice.

First, it was necessary for Americans themselves, especially the Black poor, to understand and accept their "fault" —that their failure to prosper under the system was due to some innate flaw, but a flaw which was being corrected through compensatory measures, such as special laws, programs and other benevolences that the white guardians of morality and justice thoughtfully instituted.[8]

Even when the victims of this academic diatribe do not accept its dogma, they find themselves defenseless to refute its claims. In psychological jargon there is an explanation for this which is called negative identification. The crux of this concept is that when a person is constantly identified in other than positive terms, he invariably accepts these terms and identifies with them. No doubt in Ralph's case, he had experienced a number of negative accusations, over a period of many years, and finally began to accept them as being valid. Another reason why the victim is defenseless to counter these claims is because most institutions in the Black community are controlled by whites and those not controlled by whites are influenced by them. As a result, these concepts become institutionalized and, therefore, obtain credibility. And of course there is always a cadre of Black intellectuals to sanction these concepts. While most are sincere in their convictions, being products of these same institutions, they have been trained to internalize the polemics of European culture as indelible truths. Thus, we have a situation where the victim defines the problems of his fellow victims in the terms of the victimizer.

I have attempted to provide examples of how the "blaming the victim" syndrome has been used to malign Black culture so that Blacks, even those with noble intentions, feel there is little that is positive in their culture. On the contrary, my thesis suggests that the pathological properties assigned to Black culture are, in fact, inherent to and are characteristic of European culture. It is European culture that has created the conditions in the Black community. This also holds true for the institution of slavery. The slave system did not emanate from the culture of traditional African societies, but from the cultures of Europeans. Yet we are led to believe that the forced confinement of slaves to a particular space of land (the plantation) cultivated a culture of its own that facilitated the social functions of the slaves. Frantz Fanon, the scholarly Martinique psychiatrist, challenges this view and proceeds to unravel its fallacies in his profound thesis, *Black Skin, White Masks.*

> White civilization and European culture have forced an existential deviation of the Negro. I shall demonstrate elsewhere that what is often called the black soul is a white man's artifact.[9]

Fanon then illustrates how this "artifact" effects the development of Black children.

> A normal Negro child, having grown up within a normal family, will become abnormal on the slightest contact with the white world.[10]

Simply, the abnormalities associated with the Black child vis a vis his deprived and wretched culture are in fact the syndrome of the pathology that manifest itself in European culture. Despite the research of Frantz Fanon and a few other Black scholars, who have dis-alienated Black culture from so-called slave culture, their views have not changed the antiquated thinking of most social scientists.

Mine is not a fertile revelation, W.E.B. DuBois, Edward

Blyden. George Padmore, and J.A. Rogers have all made references to African culture in their writings about Black American culture. However, it was Melville J. Herskovits who brought wide attention to the retention of "Africanisms" (African vestiges) in certain modes of Black life in *The Myth of the Negro Past*. Although Herskovits had first believed that all cultures were learned, he modified his views after seventeen years of studying different African cultures. His meticulous research revealed that Africanisms did exist, in various forms and degrees, in the culture of Black Americans as well as the cultures of Blacks who lived in the West Indies.

However, I noted that many of the preestablished modes of behavior are retained under contact, and that where cultural interchange occurs, those influence the form of what is taken over.[11]

The research model that Herskovits used and later coined for accumulating his data became known as the "ethnohistorical method." By using this method, he was able to synthesize his knowledge of African culture with history for interpreting the presence of "Africanisms" in the New World.

This conceptualization brought about a new orientation. It continued, of course, to be of paramount importance to establish African provenience of a given group as accurately as the documents permitted; to analyze, whenever possible, on the basis of the historic facts, the elements which inducted or retarded cultural change, and to utilize ethnographic field research to determine the africanisms that were present.[12]

Herskovit's findings unearthed a wealth of new information about the retention of African vestiges in the New World, and his work has since spurred others to amplify upon it and use it as a reference base. Dr. Wade Nobles, one of the pioneers in the Black psychology movement, has also researched African vestiges and gives credance to their retention in Black American culture.

With certain modifications, tribalisms have been transmitted in the form of Africanisms throughout the New World experiential periods. Cooperative effort (tribalism) was expressed in the slavery experience. The "Knights of Wise" symbolized that notion and the notion of the survival of the tribe. Funerals in contemporary black America are very symbolic of the custom of reaffirming the bonds of kinship. Distinct motor habits also have been maintained up to the present. Photographic analysis of a particular dance in the Ashanti Kwasidie rite illustrates a perfect example of the Charleston. Morality was taught in traditional times via the use of animal tales. Parables were widely prevalent during slavery—the most notable being the "brer Fox, Brer Rabbit Tales." In contemporary times, one simply notes the use of animal names to denote certain qualities. In the black communities (villages) throughout this country, women and men are referred to as "foxes, cows, bears, buzzards, dogs, and so forth." The style of talking (dramatic pauses, intonation, and the like), are all reminiscent of a people in tune with the natural rhythms of nature—in tune with the oneness of nature.[13]

As a result of this venerable thinking, the term slave culture continues to be used interchangeably with Black culture. As I will attempt to demonstrate, this amorphous culture is at best a composite of African vestiges and European culture. This composite may be analagous to the tragedy of Dr. Jeckyl and Mr. Hyde, with the latter representing European culture. My analogy is not intended to imply that African cultures were unadulterated and without any improprieties. Nor does it portend that traditional African culture exist today in any pure form. I'm not so naive to disclaim European culture's great influence on Black people; nor am I so romantic to believe Black people have retained an overwhelming portion of their traditional Africal culture. Both views, I feel, are aberrations which have no foundation, scientific or empirical. Yet, I maintain that the contemporary Black experience does contain some of the vestiges of traditional African cultures. The argument that I raise, of African vestiges surviving slavery, is indeed not a popular one. In fact, it has been the center of controversy since Africans were brought to America as slaves. But I submit that vestiges, regardless of how few or anemic they appear to be, have survived slavery, reconstruction, and exist in some forms even to this day.

Leslie A. White provides an explanation for this phenomenon in *The Science of Culture.*

We have already seen also that the human species has, by the exercise of the symbol faculty, brought a class of phenomena into existence that is, in a real sense, supra-biological or extra-somatic. These are the languages, beliefs, customs, tools, dwellings, works of art, etc. that collectively we call culture. They are supra-biological in the sense that they are transmitted by the mechanisms of social heredity; they are extra-somatic in the sense that they have an existence independent of outside just as a meteralogic force does. Every individual of the human species is born into a cultural environment as well as a natural one. And the culture into which he is born embraces him and conditions his behavior.[14]

As a student of culturology, the science of culture, White interprets cultures as a continuum which passes certain of its characteristics from generation to generation.

Let us now consider the individual in relation to the culture process. As we have noted, every individual is born into a culture that existed prior to his birth and as he grows and matures equips him with language, customs, beliefs, instruments, etc. In short, it is culture that provides him with the form and content of his behavior as a human being.[15]

White then qualifies his remarks with the following statement.

An understanding of the human mind, therefore, calls for an appreciation of the role of cultural factors as determinants of thinking feeling, and acting. The mind of the individual—the average, typical, normal individual—is as its own culture has made it.[16]

One's initial impression of White's remarks may be apprehensive and clouded with feelings that he is overstating the influence of culture. However, most of us have made statements such as: "Frenchmen are romantic," "Chinese are usually fugal," He acts just like a jew;" "Latinos are passionate," etc. At first these remarks may appear to be stereotypic (a word I dislike), and one should be discreet in how they are used. But an understanding of culturology make them plausible and not prejudicial in their intent. If such remarks can be applied to other ethnic groups, I see no reason why Black people cannot be described within the properties of their cultural matrix. When I speak of African vertiges, I'm referring to those sensory qualities which express emotions and transmit feelings; indeed, which facilitate thinking and consciousness that evolves from a common culture. How else does one explain the mutual feelings and common expression shared by Black American (Africans) and Africans from the continent and throughout the African Diaspora. In my visits to Africa, Jamaica, and Haiti, I was struck not only by the similarities in our physical appearances among the brothers I met but, more so, by the harmonious nature of our relationships.

Perhaps this is what Aime Cesaire and Leopold Senghor envisioned when they coined the concept of Negritude, or what many of us attributed to "black consciousness" in the sixties and later applied to Afro-Centrocism" in the seventies. During the writing of this book, I was grateful to learn that a Black scholar whom I highly respect has developed an ideology that embraces an Afro-Centric model for defining Black personality. Dr. Robert Williams, an innovative psychologist and originator of the BITCH test, an alternative instrument for measuring the intelligence of Black people, has named his model WEUSI, a Swahili word which means the collective Black mind.

> Accordingly, the WEUSI is conceptually defined as a collective corpus of philosophy, attitudes, preferences, values, beliefs and behavior which are at once congruous to one another and undergirded by a strong spirited rhythm and African ethos: "I am because we are and because we are, therefore, I am."[17]

In his unpublished manuscript, Dr. Williams makes a critical examination of past and present theories on personality development; explores the many facets of Black ideology, folklore and mythology; analyses a broad range of philosophical and psychological postulations; and concludes with a theory that incorporates the African ethos for understanding and defining a Black personality. In my opinion, he has written a brilliant work that should be read judiciously by all who are serious about the positive development of Black youth. Although Dr. Williams informs us that his model is not exemplary of contemporary modes of Black behavior, it is a functional and practical blueprint for the development of a new Black personality:

> Thus, the personality theory presented in this and later chapters is not a description of what is or what exists. It is a conceptualization of how a normal, healthy Black personality would develop from an African rather than from a European philosophical foundation.[18]

Dr. Williams realizes, as do other progressive thinking Black theoreticians, that further study and research needs to be undertaken to fully understand the dynamics of Black behavior. Nonetheless, his theory and those of his counterparts are a refreshing alternative to the racist diatribe espoused by most white scholars. Obviously, to continue to allow ourselves to be harnessed to theories that merely reflect the skewed reasoning of white scholars is not only detrimental to our well being but fatalistic to our existence as a people.

By this time, the reader may be asking himself what are some of the characteristics of contemporary Black behavior which are analogous to the concepts which have been discussed. Again, I must reiterate the need for further research to provide more substantive information about Black behavior. However, there does exist a few fledging studies which have identified some aspects of contemporary Black behavior that embraces the African ethos. One such study has been done by Dr. Na'm Akbar, a psychologist who has studied the unique behavior patterns of African-American children in the classroom setting. Although his study focuses on the school behavior of African-American children, I feel it also has implications for African-American youths. Dr. Akbar's findings are being presented in great detail, though not in their entirety, because I feel they are significant in helping us to appreciate the influences of African vestiges in contemporary Black behavior. To acquaint the reader with the intent of Dr. Akbar's study, his explanation is given partly:

> In this discussion we will attempt to identify some of the rather dramatic examples of behavorial patterns of the African lifestyle. Though mostly anecdotal in format, our discussion is intended to be suggestive of trends for further investigation in the light of mere attention being given to such behavorial forms and their psychic or environmental source.[19]

Dr. Akbar then proceeds to discuss six trends which are indicative of the behavioral modes in African-American children.

1. African-American Language

The African mental experience is highly affective or is one marked by considerable feeling, nor only in response to the chronic tension which characterizes the oppressed environments, but as a continuity of the high feeling tone of the African experience among African descendants throughout the world.

The African body language is a modality for maintaining rhythm in expression as well as dramatizing that which the language fails to communicate. In fact one might view the body language of the African speaker as a highly exquisite form of pantomime. One observation frequently made by non-African-American observers of African-American behavior is that there is a scarcity of communication between parents and children within the African home. This observation has been used to explain the alleged language deficits of the African-American child when in fact such an observation is a misperception of a highly intricate imbedded communication pattern.[20]

2. Oral Patterns

The importance of oral or spoken communication to the African-American lifestyle is an example of one of the many continuities with African tradition maintained in the

African-American experience. A casual observance of any community's African-American radio station will demonstrate how well developed is this skill.

Oral communication remains the predominant means of information transmission within the African-American community. Considerably more than in the broader Caucasian culture, the spoken word is relied upon much more than the written word. This emphasis on spoken communication results in a highly developed auditory or listening facility on the part of the African-American child. This child develops an acute sensitivity to subtleties in expression and intonation often unobserved by the Euro-American speaker. Consequently, the child often responds to feelings communicated in the verbal expression which may even escape the conscious notice of the speaker. There is a particular sensitivity to hostile tones which the child perceives and responds to despite efforts to veil them on the part of the speaker. It is for this reason that often African-American children respond to unexpressed prejudice and hostility on the part of non-African personnel when the personnel may perceive themselves as carefully camouflaging their feelings.

3. People Orientation

One very important element of the oral tradition which distinguishes it from the visual tradition is the centrality of a Speaker in the former case and his dispensability in the latter. This crucial difference indicates another significant characteristic of the African-American child's cultural experience. This characteristic is the considerable "people orientation" of the African culture. Experiences are significant to the degree that they relate to people in some very direct way. The charisma of many African-American heroes such as Dr. Martin Luther King, Jr., Malcolm X, and Barbara Jordan is linked to their considerable verbal eloquence. The facility of such leaders in the oral tradition serves to ignite the motivational fuse of African-Americans as they are given instruction in a familiar and forceful medium. The dual medium of the spoken word and the living person serve to motivate African people. It is interesting to note that much of the response to the orator is only incidental to the content of the message. The rhythms, the cadence of the storyteller is as important as what he is saying. For effective communication, one would hope that there exists a correlation between the rhythm and content or the message and the medium.

4. Interaction vs. Reaction

Another pattern of considerable prominence found in the African-American life experience is the interactional pattern of call-and-response. This pattern has its most dramatic examples in the Fundamentalist churches in which one finds the preacher's speech transformed into a litany of sentences and responses from the listeners. The spontaneous reactions and supportive statements of encouragement involve the speaker and listeners in a dialogue of interaction. This stands in contrast to the traditional Euro-American speaker/audience setting in which the speaker or expert dispenses wisdom and the audience listens attentively and reacts only at appropriately defined moments.[23]

5. African Thought

Because of this affective component to cognition for the African-American child, he is particularly vulnerable to his emotional reactions interfacing with his learning. His sense of being disliked by a teacher can devastate his intellectual performance. On the other hand, his sense of being liked and respected by the teacher can wrought wonderous improvements in his intellectual performance. This probably accounts for the frequent observation of rather extreme fluctuation in performance between classes for the same student. His subjective reaction to the teacher can have a rather severe effect upon his performance.

Reliance on intuition makes African-American children particularly adept in social relations because such a facility relies heavily upon empathy. In fact, the African-American child's adeptness at getting people to do what he wants them to do has frequently been described as psychopathic manipulativeness.[23]

6. Spontaneity

Another characteristic of the African-American child is his capacity to be spontaneous. His facility for easy, rapid adaptation to different situations is one of the most remarkable strengths of the African child. The capacity to respond quickly and appropriately to environmental changes facilitates the African-American child's basic comfort in most settings, where there are positive interpersonal relations.

The African-American child's spontaneity is as present in his rapid adaptation to new environments as it is in other aspects of his behavior. He is equally spontaneous with his feelings, generally responding directly and honestly.[24]

Another study that describes African influences in contemporary Black behavior is one conceived by Dr. David R. Burgest, who spent a year in East Africa studying the socialization patterns of African children. In the introduction of his study, Dr. Burgest details its purpose.

This paper is based on the premise that the values and standards by which Black children in America are reared are quite different and more than often contradictory to the values and standards of the mainstream white American society. The value orientation of Blacks in America can be traced back to original Eastern African World Outlook in the same way the value orientation dominating the White American mainstream may be traced back to original Eastern African World Outlook in the same way the value orientation dominating the White American Western World Outlook. The philosophical and ideological orientation of Black Americans, the descendants of Africans, is termed Afro-circular and the value orientation of Europeans, rooted in Western philosophical thought of early Greeks, is termed Eurolinear.[25]

A few of the highlights of his study are:

1. The Eastern African Orientation can be viewed in the African-in-America from many perspectives but first and

foremost it is hidden into his logic. One of the foremost historical and contemporary logic and thought processes under which Africans-in-America operate is "What goes around comes around." This is more than a philosophical quibble or ideological idiom. This is a way of life for the African-in-America. That is, they teach their children through experience that "what goes around comes around."

2. This Afrocircular orientation is the builder of values within a child. He soon realizes that he must have an orientation of the world which entailed "treating others as he expected to be treated or otherwise, one day may be his day."

Afrocircular child is required to live, survive and function adequately in a society where individualism, competition, and linear logic is the standard and circular logic is disregarded.[22]

Dr. Janice E. Hale is another scholar who has done extensive research on "Africanisms" (a term she uses) which exists in contemporary Black life. A list of these "Africanisms" from her book, *Black Children: Their Roots, Culture and Learning Styles* is presented in full so the reader can get a comprehensive view of their scope and function.

1. Funerals

2. Magical practices

3. Folklore (Uncle Remus stories are similar to the sacred myths of Africa.)

4. Dance

5. Song

6. Motor Habits (walking, speaking, laughing, sitting, posture, burden carrying, dancing, singing, howing, and movements made in various agricultural and industrial activities)

7. Way of dressing hair (wrapping, braiding, cornrowing)

8. Wearing of handkerchiefs, scarves (Women of the African diaspora tend to wear hair coverings more than European women. In the United States Black women wear scarves; in the Caribbean they wear bandannas, and in Africa they wear geles.)

9. Etiquette

   a. During slavery when Black people were denied titles such as Mister or Mistress, they substituted other titles of respect. Therefore, older people were called "uncle or aunt," "Brother Jones or Sister Jones."

   In African societies the ancestors are the most respected strata of the family. The elderly are the closest to the ancestors, therefore they are accorded a great deal of respect. Consequently, Black people of the diaspora have been observed to accord great respect to the elderly.

   b. Black culture encouraged turning the head when laughing place the hand over the mouth, or in speaking to elders or other respected persons averting the eyes and perhaps the face. Some people thought that when Black children turned their heads, it was a sign of inattention, but in light of their West African roots, it is interpreted to be a mark of respect.

10. Concept of time

   Black people think in terms of approximations of time rather than punctuality. An "inhouse" expression is "C.P.T."—meaning "Colored People's Time!" When a meeting is scheduled, one Black person might ask another whether they mean Eastern Standard Time or Colored People's Time. Meetings that begin on C.P. Time usually began about twenty minutes after the appointed time.

   I was amazed when travelling to West Africa and Jamaica to find a similar joke in those places about "African Times" and "Jamaican Time." Meetings that began on Jamaican time often began as much as ninety minutes after the appointed time!

11. Cooperation and sharing (Black people have expressed an orientation toward collective responsibility and interdependence.)

12. Child-rearing practices (corporal punishment, whipping, is used in disciplining children. The most common instrument is the "switch, a long, thin twig from a tree that is stripped of its leaves.)

13. Adoption of children (Black people exhibit a strong orientation toward adopting children. Robert Hill (1972) has pointed out that Black people don't go to adoption agencies to adopt children; their applications would be rejected. However, an informal system of adoption operates, wherein usually older women will provide for children when their families need assistance.

14. Myths about abnormal births in the folklore of Africa and the United States have been found to be similar.

15. Child-naming practices

16. Audience and performer styles (A highly emotional interaction exists between Black performers and audiences, with a great deal of call and responses. Usually the better known and respected the performer, the more vociferous the response. The performer will be encouraged by shouts of "Amen!," "Right-On!," "Get Down!," "Get Off!," "Take Your Time!," "Make It Plain!," and so forth depending upon whether it is a sacred and secular setting. In contrast, European-oriented audiences will indicate attention by silence, eye contact, and laughter when appropriate (Roger Abrhams, 1978).

17. Religious and spiritual expressive styles and highly emotional overtones to worship.

18. Conception of the devil.[23]

What makes Dr. Hale's research even more important is that she identifies how many of these "Africanisms" can be used to enhance the rearing and socialization of Black children. From the examples in Dr. Na'm Akbar, Dr. David Burghest, and Dr. Janice Hale's studies we can discern traces of African vestiges in contemporary Black culture. Neither of these studies should be conceived as definitive statements or be immuned from constructive criticisms, Nevertheless, they do represent a serious attempt by serious Black scholars to provide us with new understanding about Black behavior. Equally important is that they use concepts which challenge the dogma of those European scholars who feel they are authorities on Black people. What has been lacking in Black scholarship, except in rare cases, has been the Black scholar's ability to develop new theories that are based on Afro-centric, non-reactionary concepts. In their preoccupation with European thought, Black scholars have ignored the vast amount of knowledge inherent to African philosophy, tradition and culture. But if they share our concern for the positive development of Black youths it behooves them to begin to seriously consider studies by Dr. Akbar, Dr. Williams, Dr. Hale, Dr. Burghest and Dr. Nobles as cornerstones for their own professional disciplines. In this manner, these studies may begin to receive the credibility and support they deserve which are essential for institutionalization. If we are to reverse the racist doctrines which influence most institutions in the Black community, new alternatives must be provided. Institutions are the primary conveyors of culture. The church, school, social agency, etc. are the energizers for beliefs, values, and customs. They are, in fact, society's silhouettes which cast their spell on those they serve. Until these ominous silhouettes which exist in our communities are replaced, Black youths will continue to be mesmerized by an alien and warped European culture. So that a distinction can be made of the European models that presently shape and define Black culture, the basic characteristics of each will be outlined.

Deficit Model = Self Depreciation

1. Genetic inferiority
2. Pathological
3. Socially disadvantaged

4. Culturally deprived

5. Slave culture

Of all the European models the Deficit Model is the most commonly used and by far the most devastating. Its basic purpose is to denigrade Black culture and make Black people appear to be social deviants/misfits. This model is used in the institutional socialization of most Black youth and is the reason they wear the various labels associated with social and cultural deficiencies. The deficit model has a long and fixed history in the evaluation of the Black experience in America. One of its earliest examples was the inferior phrenological (brain) myth racist scientists used during slavery to prove the African had a small cranium, thus making him intellectually inferior. Another early deficiency myth was that the African lacked an organized religious system and, therefore, was a product of paganism. Such myths continued and expanded until the behavioral attributes of Black people were neatly compartmentalized into one deficit package. Today this package remains relatively secure due to the continued efforts of racist scholars to dehumanize Black people for generations yet born. The deficit model has no place in the understanding of Black behavior, and should be completely disregarded by those concerned with the positive development of Black youth.

Bi-Cultural Model = Self Diffusion

1. Slave culture

2. Assimilation

3. Sub-culture inferiority

4. Ethological modification

5. European/mainstream domination

6. Integration

This model attempts to express the broad diversities in racial and ethnic groups, suggesting that they can all mutually survive in an integrated society. Perhaps this model does have merit for other ethnic and racial groups. The advocates for this model, mainly so-called white liberals and misguided Blacks, claim that it allows Black people to cherish parts of their own culture and, at the same time, adopt the values of the dominant European culture. This may not be entirely true all the time but history has shown that any form of integration/assimilation has always meant the compromising of Black priorities to accommodate the so-called white majority. On the surface, this model is somewhat representative of the manner in which different ethnic groups do function in this society. These groups do hold on to their ethnicity and are able to "mainstream" into the larger, dominant culture. And I'm not so naive to romanticize that Black people can function, with any reasonableness, in this society without interacting with other groups and conforming to certain social or legal sanctions. However, this model, no matter how it is modified, is unable to accept Black culture as equal to other cultures. It still carries with it many of the characteristics of the deficit model. We have witnessed too many examples of Blacks who have been successful in negotiating two cultures. But to preserve their success, they usually find they are expected to eventually forsake their own culture. As a result, the bi-cultural model imposes an intra-group scale for Blacks, i.e., Negro, Uncle Tom, Black, Nationalist, etc., which rates them according to their propensity to adopt European values. This type of cultural diffusion only creates divisiveness, individualism, and sectarianism, all of which ignores the collective development of the Black masses. Though advocates of the bi-cultural model disclaim it is "conflict oriented," the very nature of American society promotes and endorses racial conflict. We do not live in a "Camelot" society, and therefore, Black people must develop and strengthen their own "character" to survive and prosper as a people. The bi-cultural model has no place in the construction of this character.

Neither of these models acknowledge the vestiges of African culture nor do they promote a collective sense of Black awareness and Black self-determination. These models have been conceived by European scholars who are determined to maintain their self-acclaimed status as authorities on Black behavior. To allow these models to continue to define how we do or should not function will forfeit any hope we have to determine our own destiny. We have already permitted these models to penetrate our psyches to the point of almost total endoctrination. Yet we can still escape this mind control if we begin to adopt theories of Black scholars like Dr. Nobles, Dr. Akbar, Dr. Hale, Dr. Burghest and Dr. Williams. Their theories not only refute European diatribe but more importantly establishes new constructs for understanding Black behavior. And central to these new constructs is the recognition of an Afro-Centric view based on African thought, African religion, African cosmology, African psychology and African culture. It is this view, Afrocentricism, which will enable Black people to raise themselves above the academic dogma that insults our intelligence. In his thought provoking book, *Afrocentricity: The Theory of Social Change*, Molefi Kite Asante provides an incisive analysis of Afrocentricity. Afrocentricity is the centerpiece of human regeneration. To the degree that it is incorporated into the lives of the millions of Africans on the continent and in the diaspora, it will become revolutionary. It is purposeful, giving a true sense of destiny based on the facts of history and experience. Although Afrocentricity is still in its embryonic stage, we already have sufficient information to put it into an operational model. Some of the characteristics of this model would be as follows:

Afro-Centric Model = Collective Self Realization
and Black Liberation

1. African Vestiges
2. Nationalism
3. Pan Africanism
4. Ethnological Superiority
5. African Psychology & Cosmology
6. Collective Consciousness

The Afro-Centric Model would provide Black youths a view of themselves, their community and relationships with others which transcends the academic diatribe of white scholars and give them a positive perspective of Black life. Instead of shaping their lives from the self-defeating models assigned to them by whites, they would mold their behavior from the self-fulfilling matrix of Afro-Centric ideology. An Afro-Centric

Model would help Black youths have a clearer understanding of the social forces that impede their development and give them a collective identity and a common destiny. In addition it would provide three essential qualities which are fundamental to the positive development of a people. These qualities are: 1) a sense of identity; 2) a sense of history; and 3) a sense of struggle. A brief description of each will identify why they are so crucial.

SENSE OF IDENTITY

A knowledge and appreciation of one's true identity is paramount to the development of a positive personality. It is the springboard for understanding one's kinship with his own people and relationships with other groups. This is especially true of an oppressed people whose knowledge of their true identity incites grave concern by their oppressor.

It is dangerous to speak seriously of the power of identity in the presence of an oppressed and colonized people . . . even if the ultimate issues are camouflaged by vague and seemingly harmless references to cultural ramifications. For the movement among non-white peoples toward authentic identity is the starting point of all struggle against those imposed structures of a dominating society which warp the vision of our manhood . . .[24]

The identity of Blacks in America has undergone numerous social and psychological transformations, i.e., slave, nigger, Negro, colored, Black, etc. This confusion derives mainly from the lack of a viable cultural model which would be the source for defining one's true identity. The Afro-Centric Model helps to dissolve this confusion because it stems from a monolithic African sensibility. Thus the prefix African to one's citizenship status (America) would appear to be a logical progression in the establishment of one's true identity (African American). It is not the intent of this commentary to impose a new name on Black people. Such an attempt would necessitate the writing of another book to dispel the anxieties that normally surface whenever this name is suggested. I have only cited this example because I sincerely feel that some day Black Americans will see its validity and embrace it with affection and reverence. The acceptance of an Afro-Centric Model as a matrix for our identity will be the catalyst for making this decision inevitable.

SENSE OF HISTORY

It has been said that a race without knowledge of its history is a race without understanding of its roots. The institution of American slavery understood this axiom and systematically attempted to destroy the history of its African slaves. And when it was not successful in destroying this history, it did everything it could to distort it. The history of Black people in America has been so suppressed that today thousands of Black youths are completely ignorant of their past. Instead, the history they learn is one of the most racist interpretations of human events that exist anyplace in the world. It is a history that has made heroes out of white racists, justified the existence of slavery, branded Africa as an uncivilized nation, and maligned the deeds of Black freedom fighters. Simply, the oppressor defines history to justify his oppression, but as Lerone Bennett states, "it is a matter of life and death to the oppressed, who cannot find themselves or free themselves without first finding and freeing their history." The knowledge of history becomes fundamental to everything we do. To quote Lerone Bennett again:

> It is a living library which provides a script of roles and models to which growth can aspire. By telling us who we are, history tells us what we can do. By telling us where we have been, history tells us where we can go.[25]

Few Black youth have any real perception of where they are going. Consequently, they identify with almost any trend that has popular appeal. This is not entirely their fault and we should not expect them to do anything else so long as their knowledge of history is flawed by lies and distortions.

SENSE OF STRUGGLE

Last but not least, we should provide Black youth with a sense of struggle. Frederick Douglass, the great Black orator, once said:

The whole history of the progress of human liberty shows that all concessions, yet made to her august claims have been born of earnest struggle.[26]

It should be clear to all Black people, by now, that significant progress will not be made without significant struggle. Yet many Black people continue to ignore this reality and act as though some fairy godmother sent from the heavens will give them freedom. Nothing can be more ridiculous. We must teach Black youth how to struggle; what it actually is; and what it is not. Too often Black youths have a misconception about struggle and rely on their physical attributes to deal with problems instead of their mental abilities. Let us not be mistaken about what I mean by struggle. Struggle at this point in our history means the development of the mind and self-discipline. Without these two factors, I seriously doubt if we would ever be able to have a significant impact on our oppressor. Black youth must not be tempted or encouraged to pursue acts of violence that will only lead to their destruction. They must be taught that the behavior and attitudes of Black youths become important if they are to assume their place in the struggle for Black liberation. The crisis of Black youth is, in fact, only a reflection of the crisis that besets Black adults. This is not to imply Black youths have no unique problems. However, because Black youths are more visible and vulnerable, their problems become magnified to such a degree we are led to believe they are the greatest barriers to Black liberation. As a result, many Black adults become overly critical and even fearful of Black youths who, in turn vent their frustrations and hostilities on the Black community. A vicious cycle takes place that pits youths against adults and neither seem able to resolve its consequences. However, until both groups begin to see similarities in their problems and collectively seek out solutions to them, the Black community will continue to engage itself in an intragroup struggle that has become the hallmark of oppressed people. Black youths must learn what our struggle is about and learn to use their energies in support of it. An Afro-Centric model will give Black youths "a sense of struggle" that is so conspicuously absent in much of their behavior today.

Having an acquisition of these "senses" will provide Black youth nourishment to enhance their development, thus enhancing the future of Black people. I realize that much of what I'm suggesting may appear to some to be idealistic. And others may feel it is unattainable. But these words are only relative to what we are willing to commit our energies to achieve. If your vision is clouded by a lack of desire and commitment than my suggestions have no merit. If, on the other hand, your vision is illuminated by a burning desire to be liberated—then my suggestions can become seeds for harvesting future generations. To those whose vision is blurred by pessimism and/or indifference, I would suggest they quit reading this commentary and try to get their refund. But for those who still have hope, as I do, then we must begin now to plant the seeds that will reap a new harvest. And these seeds must not be saturated with social pesticides that will interfere with their natural development. They must be nourished with the fertile waters of our ancient rivers and the revealing sunshine of our ancestors' wisdom.

We are not a new people on the face of this earth. Our history reaches back to the earliest man. Why then should we not look to our past and reap from it that which is meaningful and still relevant to our contemporary existence. To completely forsake it would be like preparing our coffins, anticipating the final dirges. Let us begin to nourish a harvest that will enrich the lives of our future generations. And as the great poet, Margaret Walker, proclaimed, "Let a new race of men now take control."

CHAPTER THREE

SOCIALIZATION IN A HOSTILE ENVIRONMENT: THE CRISIS OF BLACK ADOLESCENCE

> The manchild (and womanchild) of 1984 must be convinced that there is reason for hope. He must be made to understand that the quality of life does improve as he grows older, that everything falls into place as adults approach 'age of enlightenment.'
>
> Claude Brown

When Kunta Kente was kidnapped from his native country of Juffure, Gambia in West Africa and taken to the alien environment of America, his orderly pattern of socialization was dramatically altered. No longer did he have the support of the social systems which were inherent to his traditional culture that prepared him for adulthood. As a captive, Kunta Kente and millions of his youthful counterparts were resocialized to serve the interest of a dehumanizing slave system that impaired their normal development. As a result of this resocialization, Black youths have never had an opportunity to develop their true potential in an environment free of racism and social oppression. Instead, Black youths have had to shape their character from an environment that was antithetical to their welfare and which violated the traditional practices associated with the rearing of African children. Although Black youths have, over the years, learned to adjust to this oppressive environment, it has not been without great sacrifice and the compromising of their natural patterns of socialization. If we are to, however, harvest a generation of Black youth who will have a greater chance to achieve their true potential, we must help them to overcome the pervasive racism and oppression which impairs their natural development. This will not be an easy task, for the obstacles to this goal are seemingly overwhelming and deeply rooted in the American way of life. But these obstacles must be uprooted and replaced with seeds that will sprout new vistas and provide Black youths with positive alternatives to the social malaise they are now exposed to. The challenge that I present is fundamental to the liberation of Black people, for it raises the question whether it is possible to reap the harvest I envision from a land that is contaminated with racism and other social pollutants. In other words, can Black youths be expected to develop their true potential under a system of racism and oppression that imposes undue hardships and emotional strain on their character?

In the early forties, the American Youth Commission partially addressed this problem by sponsoring a series of studies to "see whether Negro youth faced distinctive problems in their development as individual personalities." I use the word partially to describe these studies because they did not fully examine the effects of racism and oppression on the personality development of Black youth. Instead, they conformed to the research models developed by Robert Parks, dean of the Chicago School of Sociology, that had gained broad acceptance as the foremost methodologies for studying social problems. As a result, these studies were preoccupied with social stratification, class distinctions, and victim analysis instead of focusing on the psychological damage that stemmed from racism and social oppression. Nevertheless, these studies were important because they involved many of our leading Black social scientists of that period. E. Franklin Frazier, Allison Davis, Charles Johnson, and Walter A. Adams were all major researchers in these studies which focused on the personality development of "Negro" youth in four different geographic environments. The studies in this series were:

Children of Bondage: The Personality of Negro Youth in the Urban South, by Allison Davis and John Dollard.

Negro Youth at the Crossways: The Personality Development in the Middle States by E. Franklin Frazier.

Growing Up in the Black Belt: Negro Youth in the Rural South, by Charles Johnson.

Color and Human Nature: Negro Personality Development in a Northern City, by W. Lloyd Warner, Buford H. Junker and Walter A. Adams.

In researching the personality development of Black youths, the researchers used case histories to document their findings but were careful to indicate their studies should not be interpreted as being representative of all Black youth. Yet even with this qualification, these studies did draw some general conclusions about Black youths which can be summarized as follows:

1. That the double standards imposed by America's system of caste (racism) definitely had a debilitating effect on the personality development of Black youth;
2. That Black youths did not have equal access to the proper resources and institutions that were necessary to help them enter the mainstream of American society;

3. That class status within the Black community played an important role in how successful Black youths were in adjusting to the double standards of American life. The higher a youth was on the social ladder, the easier it was for him/her to make this adjustment;

4. To compensate for their inequities, Black youth often develop personalities that induced maladjusted behavior.

Around the same period, two other studies were published that attempted to explain the impact of an oppressed environment on the personality development of Black people. The first study, Mydal's hallmark analysis of Black-white relations, *An American Dilemma*, confirmed, in much greater detail, many of the findings reported in the American Youth Commission's studies. The second study, however, Kariner Kardiner and Oversey's much ballyhooed *Mark of Oppression*, did little more than provide a victim analysis approach in identifying 26 stereotypic characteristics the authors alleged Blacks to have as the result of being oppressed.

In 1950, the *Journal of Negro Education*, published by Howard University, featured a special issue which further examined the personality development of Black youth under the title, "The Negro Child and Youth in the American Social Order." This issue contained an impressive number of essays by such noted Black scholars as Benjamin E. Mays, Horace Mann Bond, Kenneth Clark, Robert Weaver, as well as E. Franklin Frazier. One article from this volume, written by Ira De A. Reid, summarizes the general consensus expressed by the various writers;

1. The systematic subordination of Negroes to whites in the American social system has a discernible effect upon the socialization of the Negro.

2. The present racial organization of the American social system is a direct outgrowth of that subordination.

3. The resultant racial organization tends to provide for its members an escape from (and compensations for) the domination of the wider society, creating new values deemed essential to the Negro group's survival.

4. Thus, the socialization of the American Negro takes place in two general areas of social interaction, the one broadly cultural, the other narrowly racial, in neither of which is the process of socialization effected with other than marginal completeness and satisfaction.[1]

In a more recent study of this problem, Leon W. Chestang identifies three conditions which shape character development in what he calls "a hostile environment."

Three conditions, socially determined and institutionally supported, characterize the black experience: social injustice, societal inconsistency, and personal impotence. To function in the face of any one of them does cruel and unusual violence to the personality. To function in the face of all three subjects the personality to severe crippling or even destruction. These three crucial conditions, however, confront the black person throughout his life, and they determine his character development.[2]

These conditions, then, contribute to two forms of behavior which as Chestang notes.

. . . resulted in the development of two parallel and opposing thought structures—each based on values, norms, and beliefs supported by attitudes, feelings and behaviors—that imply feelings of depreciation on the one hand and a push for transcendence on the other.[3]

Thus, the depreciated character seeks mainly to survive in a hostile environment while the transcendent character advocates a universal affinity with the "inalienable rights of man," and therefore, challenges the hostile environment.

. . . the transcendent differentiates itself from the depreciated by this central trait. The depreciated will sell its soul to survive, the transcendent will give its life to be.[4]

Chestang's thesis provides a basis for understanding the psychological dynamics that must be taken into account when developing a model for the positive development of Black youth. We can assume from Chestang's thesis that the degree to which a person adopts a depreciated character or a transcendent character is contingent upon his personal coping skills; set of values, resiliency to adversity; and level of self esteem. Irrespective of these qualities, however, it is highly likely that every Black person has developed what Thomas J. Edwards calls psychological scar tissue.

It is doubtful that any Black American is totally free from this scarring. As we become scarred in different ways, so we have our own unique and private ways of reacting to the slings and arrows of outrageous racism.[5]

The medication used by Black people to treat these scars is analogous to the following forms of behavior:

Adaptive Behavior
accepts status in life and tries to make the most of it.

becomes indoctrinated to the Blame the Victim syndrome.

develops a passive attitude towards racism.

Modified Behavior
modifies values to be more acceptable to whites.

strives to achieve status within the norms and values of the Black community and dominant white society vis a vis Du Bois' double consciousness.

Compensated Behavior
seeks to compensate for oppressed status by attempting to oppress members of his own race.

often becomes a victim of drugs, alcohol, and other forms of escapism.

The above patterns of behavior are not in themselves atypical of the manner in which most people adapt to their environment. But for people who are being victimized by oppression these patterns of behavior do little to counteract its adverse influence. To merely be able to cope with oppression only sustains and perpetuates its existence. In building a model for the positive development of Black youth, we must be concerned with helping them to neutralize and eventually overcome racism and oppression. This must be our ultimate goal if we really desire to achieve our true potential as a people and as individuals. Dr. Frances Welsing makes note of this goal in discussing what she calls the trappings of "white supremacy maintenance."

> Black and other non-white peoples ultimately seeking not simply their survival but their maximal development, must therefore compensatorily establish as their highest specific goal and value; the maximal development of themselves by *whatever means necessary* will be extracted from them as the white supremacy system seeks to maintain itself to continue the status quo.[6]

According to Dr. Welsing, the maximum development of Black people will never be fully realized until we are completely free from the yoke of racism and oppression.

> ...there can be no truly functional mental health for peoples of color, meaning patterns of logic, thought, concepts, speech, action and emotional response outside of the practice of counter-racism as long as the system of white supremacy domination remains the major world reality.[7]

Although Dr. Welsing's perceptions may not mirror mass opinion, they do cause us to take a closer examination of ourselves. Dr. Welsing's comments may appear to be overly dramatic to some because we take pride in the many Blacks who have become successful and famous despite being products of an oppressive environment. Many of their achievements appear to completely defy the trappings of racism and oppression. While this may be marginally true, the problem with this reasoning is that we will never know how much greater their achievements might have been if they had not been products of a racist environment. Then, too, a strong case can be made that even though we have had a significant number of successful and famous people, many of these people have not always acted in the best interest of the Black community. What we are advocating is not just a generation of successful people but a generation of people who are committed to liberating the race and raising it to the heights it is capable of achieving. This will not be an easy task. The socialization of adolescence has always been a nebulous process. And for Black youths, it has constituted a perpetual crisis. To acquire a better understanding of the dynamics of adolescence, a brief view of its origin will be necessary.

Throughout the early history of man, adolescence was an amorphous period with no distinct characteristics to differentiate it from childhood or adulthood. Humans were simply categorized as being either children or adults, and there was no middle period to transform the former to the latter. One explanation for this void is given by Victoria Secunda:

> In ancient times, age gradation did not exist because there was so little of life to be divided up according to chronology. Life expectancy was once brief indeed: Prehistoric people could expect to live no more than eighteen years. In Roman times, people lived, on an average, to age twenty-two. Between twenty and thirty years of life were allotted people in medieval times.[8]

It was not until the seventeenth century, with the publication of *Emile*, Jean Jacques Rousseau's pedagogical treatise on man's quest for education and moral affirmation, did adolescence begin to acquire an identity that distinguished it from childhood and adulthood. In his voluminous allergorical novel, Rousseau traces the moral and educational enlightenment of Emile from infancy to adulthood. Emile's efforts to attain self discovery during his formative years are thwarted by the state which regulates and controls the information he so desperately seeks. Only when he reaches the age of 15 does Emile become exposed to the teachings of life, and is able to begin his transformation to adulthood. Rousseau believed it was during the ages of 15 to 20 that a person was enlightened and called this period adolescence.

While Rousseau is considered by most to be the father of "adolescence," it was the work of E. Stanley Hall that crystallized it into a concrete form. Hall's two volume treatise, *Adolescence, Its Psychology and Its Relations to Physiology, Anthropology, Sociology, Sex, Crime, Religion and Education* established the thesis that adolescence was the "last great wave" and "second birth" which prepared man to fulfill his destiny. The works of Rousseau and Hall were later amplified by Sigmund Freud who was largely responsible for uncovering the sexuality of adolescence. Another major work that helped shape the character of adolescence was Erik H. Erikson's *Childhood and Society*. This classic work interprets the human development cycle more within a social context than the philosophical and sexual writings of Rousseau and Hall. In doing so, Erikson focuses on the formation of identity as being the determinant for shaping one's future.

Adolescence is the age of the final establishment of a dominant positive ego identity. It is then that a future within reach becomes part of the conscious life plan. It is then that the question arises whether or not the future was anticipated in earlier expectations.[9]

Despite the revelations of Rousseau, Hall, Freud, and Erikson, adolescence was slow to become widespread among the masses, and was primarily reserved for the elite as described by Louise J. Kaplan.

In Western societies, as in some hunger-gathering societies and in all the ancient civilizations, the time to adolescent, or "grow up into adulthood," was originally granted exclusively to young men of the upper classes and to a few intellectual, religious, artistic, or otherwise gifted girls and boys.[10]

With the emancipation of the working class during the early twentieth century, the "privilege" of being an adolescent became more universal. But this universality was not without its problems for it forced society to modify its institutions to accommodate the masses of youths who were now entitled to the privileges associated with adolescence. The childhood years were no longer the link to adulthood and social systems and institutions were obligated to prepare the adolescents to become this connection. In early America, however, the emergence of adolescence had been retarded because as a fledgling nation the colonists relied heavily on its young to perform adult responsibilities. During the Revolutionary and Civil Wars youth were drafted in the militia, sometimes as young as 12 years old, and were pressed to be adults regardless of their maturity or skills. As a nation entangled in war over slavery, a ruptured economy, and expansion, America did not hesitate to deplore its youths as soldiers, field hands, and builders. As America resolved these issues, it began to see its youths as a distinct population with special needs. Still in the late nineteenth century, the status of adolescence in America was subject to interpretation, state laws and cultural biases. For example, during the Industrial Revolution, youths continued to be called upon to do adult work and literally labored as serfdoms in the mills and factories which were spearheading America's thrust into economic prominence. Then, too, there was no distinction made between crimes committed by youths from those committed by adults. As a consequence, youths were processed under the same laws as adults until 1899 when Chicago inaugurated the country's first juvenile court which later became the model for similar courts of law. And though it was deemed appropriate for youths 17 and over to serve in the military, they were not entitled to vote, purchase liquor or participate in activities designated "for adults only." The problem of stabilizing and defining the period of adolescence was not due to its relationship to childhood but rather due to its relationship to adulthood. The end of childhood could be determined by puberty but there were no pronounced physical changes to signal the beginning of adulthood. And so the period of adolescence remained somewhat of an enigma, and youths fluctuated between childhood and adulthood almost until the advent of World War I. Indeed adolescence in America has been and still is a period which is clouded with contradictions, uncertainties and a myriad of social problems.

Although this brief review of the evolution of adolescence is basically a reflection of western civilization, it is relevant to this commentary because regardless of what dislikes we may have of western civilization, our Black youths are greatly influenced by its properties and values. We must always bear in mind the paradox we live under because in shaping a new generation of Black youths we cannot disregard our attachment to western civilization. Although Black youths are subjected to double standards, they are, nonetheless, characterized by the same classifications as white youths. And these classifications have developed from a world view that has been absorbed in every facet of American life. In discussing the status of Black youths, we have little choice but to discuss it from this frame of reference. Thus, we must use this frame of reference to understand the problems that are unique to Black adolescents if we are to cultivate a new harvest for them. One concept that is attributed to this frame of reference and which plays an important role in assessing adolescent development is the formulation of developmental tasks best popularized by the model conceived by Robert Havighurst. Havighurst believed that adolescents had to achieve certain tasks if they were to successfully meet the challenges of adulthood. Furthermore, he believed the failure to achieve a particular task would later result in the adolescent having a deficiency during adulthood. Havighurst's developmental tasks thus became the standard for measuring the ability of adolescents to transcend into adulthood. The developmental tasks conceived by Havighurst were as follows:

1. Achieve new and more mature relations with agemates of both sexes.
2. Achieving a masculine or feminine social role.
3. Accepting one's physique and using the body effectively.
4. Achieving emotional independence of parents and other adults.
5. Preparing for marriage and family life.
6. Preparing for an economic career.
7. Acquiring a set of values and an ethical system as a guide to behavior—developing an ideology.
8. Desiring and achieving socially responsible behavior.

I do not have an argument against any of Havighurst's developmental tasks. From a developmental perspective, each appears to be a reasonable expectation for measuring the maturity of adolescents. What I am critical of is that they do not fully assess the unique needs of Black adolescents to achieve what I feel is necessary for their adulthood. Although there are universal properties governing all adolescents, Black adolescents have special needs which necessitate their mastery of additional tasks to counter the pervasive racism they are subjected to. Because of their special needs, I believe we must extend the developmental tasks for Black adolescents. I have identified below five tasks which I believe should be included in this extension. I call these tasks "Liberating Tasks" in contrast to the traditional name of developmental tasks. Liberation should be the top priority for Black people and the achievement of traditional developmental tasks by Black adolescents fall far short of preparing them to meet this challenge.

Liberating Tasks for Black Adolescents

1. Achieving a sense of identity that embraces the culture, history, and struggles of people of African descent.
2. Achieving a strong sense of racial pride.
3. Developing an ideology based on Pan African principles.
4. Developing an Afro-Centric view of the world.
5. Acquiring a Black value system.

These tasks are not intended to be finite or immuned to criticism. I realize that developmental tasks are normally cycled through scientific methodologies to test their reliability and credibility. But this commentary does not profess to be a scientific document and the urgency of my concerns do not allow time to collect quantifiable data and do longitudinal studies. On the other hand, I hope that the liberating tasks I have identified might spur research by Black social scientists to assess their usefulness. It should be obvious by now that we cannot continue to rely solely on traditional theories to improve our conditions and enhance our status as a people. As I have enunciated again and again, this is the responsibility of Black people. Admittedly it will be difficult to reap a bountiful harvest from contaminated soil, but we have always been a creative people with the ability to adapt to and modify even the most painful of situations.

Obviously, if the period of adolescence has been traumatic for white youth, it is axiomatic that it has been a perpetual crisis for Black youths. As I have discussed in Chapter one, Black youths were held to be prize possessions during slavery. Generally after the age of 12 they were expected to perform as adults. Few if any experienced the privileges of adolescence. To be sure, the manchild which Claude Brown wrote about in his startling autobiographical novel, *Manchild In the Promised Land*, was not born in the streets of Harlem but in the pliant cotton fields of antebellum Georgia, South Carolina, and Mississippi. And even when Black youths reached the chronological age of adulthood, they continued to be treated like children. The system of American racism and oppression has found it convenient and self serving to treat Blacks as children because it helped to massage the racist egoes of whites and give them the illusion of being superior. To racist America, Blacks have always been children and the period of adolescence for Black youths was coerced by a conscious effort to disrupt their socialization. Contrary to the contemporary belief that Black youths are becoming "an endangered species." I contend that they have always been an "endangered species." One way to demoralize a people is to infect its youth with every imaginable social disease so when or if they do reach adulthood, they are a hopeless generation of cripples—in mind, body, and spirit.

Let it be clearly understood that in the context in which I'm discussing the status of Black adolescents, I'm not referring to how they are perceived by the Black community. The Black community places great value on its youth even though it has not always had the resources to reinforce this concern. This was particularly true in the South where Black youths were generally manageable and seldom violated community sanctions. Black parents, being ever conscious of the evils of racism, did everything possible to protect their sons and daughters and train them to behave within the boundaries acceptable to whites. They understood that Black youths had to walk a narrow line to buffer the overt racism which was prevalent in the South. Those youths who crossed this line were chastised not only by their parents but by other adults in the community. The management and nurturing of Black youths were considered to be a community responsibility which incorporated some customs associated with traditional African societies. Unfortunately these customs began to erode for those Black families which migrated North in significant numbers at the turn of the twentieth century. The dramatic transition to urban life found most Black families ill equipped to cope with its mayhem and crisis-oriented living conditions.

Hollis R. Lynch describes this transition as follows:

The Negro has little developed aptitude for the commercial and industrial requirements of city life. A rural people can remain embalmed, as it were, in a state of nature almost indefinitely. But if transferred to the city, they are forced into a life and death struggle with the powers of destruction.[11]

As a result, the customs akin to Black families in the South began to dissipate and were replaced with customs that were contrary to the traditions which had previously enabled them to maintain some semblance of stability. The tradition of the Black community collectively rearing its young was now assigned to individual families to perform this function. But this became a difficult task for most Black families because of the diffusion in family life that was brought on by economic strain. The fragmentation of the Black family in urban communities placed greater pressure on Black youths to develop their own coping skills which they required from the Street Institution.

By the end of World War II, Black youths had become inflicted with all of the trappings of urban living, and the Street Institution became, for most, their primary reference for survival. One of the most revealing accounts of Black youths surviving in the Street Institution is recorded by Claude Brown in his highly acclaimed autobiography. Although Brown's narrative may be somewhat over dramatic, it does provide a graphic reference for examining the effects of urban life on some Black youths. One account from Brown's narrative highlights the importance of a youth acquiring a "reputation."

In our childhood, we all had to make our reputations in the neighborhood (Street Institutions). Then we'd spend the rest of our lives living up to them. A man was respected on the basis of his reputation. The people in the neighborhood whom everybody looked up to were cats who'd killed somebody. The little boys in the neighborhood whom the adults respected were the little boys who didn't let anybody mess with them.[12]

Somehow Claude Brown managed to escape the Street Institution of Harlem and eventually earned a degree in law. On a recent excursion to Harlem, Brown reveals that not much had changed for Black youths—but had, in fact, worsened.

The unimaginably difficult struggle to arrive at a productive manhood in urban America is more devastatingly monstrous than ever before. All street kids are at least semi-abandoned, out on those mean streets for the major portion of the day and night. They are at the mercy of a cold-blooded and ruthless environment; survival is a matter of fortuity, instinct, ingenuity and unavoidable conditioning. Consequently, the manchild who survives is usually more cunning, more devious and often more vicious than his middle class counterpart. These traits are the essential contents of his survival kit.[13]

Of course Brown's incisive observation is not typical of all Black youths; nonetheless, the fact that it is descriptive of even a few should be of grave concern to every Black person. As I have already noted, many Black youths had to assume the responsibility for their own socialization that resulted in them adopting life styles which were compatible with the tarnished fabric of the Street Institution. One commentary on these adoptive life styles is reported in a study of sixty-one Black male youths who lived in the Boston ghetcolony of Roxbury from 1967 to 1974. The study was called Project Pathway and its purpose is described by its principle researchers.

Specifically, we wanted to repaint one of social science's most blurry and unarticulated portraits—the image of the poor northern urban black teenager—splitting the undifferentiated profile into a series of pictures of complex, changing individuals. We wanted to comprehend how the black teenager saw his own range of options, and how he developed strategies for getting what he wanted out of life.[14]

The researchers concluded that their subjects could be categorized by the following coping strategies:

—Keeping cool - Strongly motivated by material things
—Going under - Lacking in self confidence

—Keeping close - Barely making it
—Staying clean - Trying to be straight
—Getting over - Making it anyway possible
—Hiding out - Retreating from reality

These strategies can be interpreted as the means by which some Black youth cope with adolescence and further suggest that their socialization is largely dependent on their own initiative. Conspicuously absent is a systematic and organized process to ensure that each youth receives the orientation and training to function within a social matrix which fosters constructive behavior. On the contrary, the strategies adopted by these youths are reactionary in their function and void of influence from socializing institutions such as the family, church, and school.

> As a means of socialization, it (Street Institution) offers only a limited number of roles to local youngster, particularly males. And of course, the more entrapped they become, seeking fulfillment in the few opportunities and roles available.[15]

Black girls tend to rely on other strategies to facilitate their adolescence. Unlike Black boys, who develop their own means of coping, girls generally choose to emulate adult models who they can identify with. Joyce Ladner discusses this process.

> There was much concern as to what kind of woman one should become, and this subject is addressed when girls are still pre-adolescents. There were a number of role models in their immediate environment who were used as sources of identification. In a few cases girls chose not to be like any of these models but to be either like someone beyond their environs (such as an actress or singer) or like no one they knew. Therefore, images of what kind of woman one should be took a variety of forms. Conceptions of emerging womanhood are transmitted from generation to generation. Although there were a variety of role models for these girls to choose from, they were still restricted, more or less, to emulating and following certain patterns of their mothers and other women in their immediate environ-

ment. Thus, there were often pervasive influences which they experienced within the home and community, even if they did aspire to more higher in the social class hierarchy.[16]

The most common models which girls in Ladner's study aspired to be like were the following:

—Hard Working Woman
—Middle Class Woman
—Strongly Independent Woman
—Carefree Woman
—Highly Motivated and Resourceful Woman

The difference between urban Black girls and boys preparing themselves for adulthood is that girls are more likely to model their behavior from adults while the life styles of boys emerge from the experiences they have in coping with their environment. This is not to suggest Black boys are not influenced by adult models, but their life styles are shaped more by situations and events than by other people. While both Black girls and boys are also influenced by peers, this influence is relative in that the influence peers have on each other is predicated on who or what has influenced them. Most likely they are all influenced by the same sources, and peer influence simply reinforces dominant behavioral norms and modes of life styles.

PUBERTY AND BLACK ADOLESCENCE

Despite their varied interpretations about the properties of adolescence, most social scientists will agree that it begins with puberty. The real significance of puberty, then, is that it is the front end of the adolescent crisis. David Elkind collaborates this fact in his work, *All Grown Up and No Place To Go*:

Young people begin to worry when they become capable of anticipating the future (a product of formal operational thinking), and puberty provides not one but rather a whole series of matters to worry about. As soon as one issue is resolved, another takes its place. If teenagers are not worried about height, they are worried about weight; if not menstruation, then breast size; and so on. Puberty presents teenagers with a series of unknown changes, and each one constitutes a peril of puberty.

Worrying about the perils of puberty is a symptom of the stress connected with defining a personal identity. When a girl worries about whether she will ever get her period, she is concerned about being different from her friends who have already "got it." Similarly, a boy who worries about being short is worrying about being different from the norm of attractiveness, strength, and masculinity. He worries about not being included in sports, about being treated as younger than his peers, and about being called names such as "Shorty." The changes associated with puberty are overwhelmingly stressful because they confront the teenager with so many questions difficult to answer.[17]

Among Black youths the problem of puberty is most likely to be more serious because I believe Black youths are more ignorant about puberty (and subsequently about sex) than their white counterparts. As a result, most Black youths enter puberty with little understanding of its functions and proceed to learn about sex from whatever sources they find which usually comes from the Street Institution. Black parents may inform their daughters about the virtues of chastity and warn their sons to be careful if they have intercourse, but there is generally no formal sex education given to either. Robert Staples draws a similar conclusion.

From the limited data on the subject, it is apparent that black parents are not the source of sex education for most black youths. The majority of them, in fact, receive their initial knowledge of sex from peers and other sources. And, much of that information is fragmented and inaccurate.[18]

The misinformation acquired by many Black youths during puberty is largely responsible for their sometimes reckless sexual behavior and the strained relationships between males and females. When young people are ignorant about puberty and the functions of sex, they are more prone to abuse themselves and others, both physically and emotionally. Sex begins to play an increasingly and more prominent role in the lives of young people when they have reached puberty.

The dominant theme of the ego states of adolescence is sexual, and it becomes more sexual as the child gets closer to adulthood. During late adolescence, sexual elements color attitudes more than ever and become an inherent aspect of the identity sense.[19]

As the "identity sense" becomes solidified during adolescence, youths begin to establish their sexual behavior which, in turn, influences their moral behavior.

Undoubtedly, gender-role expectations represent the most powerful factor shaping adolescent sexual behavior. A violation of fundamental gender-role expectations is a violation of the moral order. Sexual behavior, then, is more than just gender-significant behavior, it is also moral behavior.[20]

Since sexuality begins to mature during adolescence, a concerted effort should be made to provide Black youth with a positive attitude toward sex. What I'm suggesting is that Black youths have an official "rites of passage" at the onset of puberty to prepare them for positive sex roles during their adolescence. By adopting positive sex roles during this period, I believe most will develop a greater appreciation of their bodies and of bodies to which they interact. Also, the acquisition of positive sex roles will contribute to their "self discovery" and help them to fully appreciate the real purpose and beauty of sex. The generation that we must begin to harvest need to be free of as many misconceptions about the nature of life as possible. Sex is an indispensable quality of life's developmental cycle, and therefore, should be a critical component to the foundation we must build for the positive development of Black youths.

PEPSI GENERATION SYNDROME

Other problems which contribute to the crisis in Black adolescence can be lumped under what I call the Pepsi Generation Syndrome. I use this commercialized term simply as a means to describe the generation that was an outgrowth of the surge for independence and social reform that typified the youth movements in the sixties. Bearing the renaissance names of "flower Children," "sun children," and politically dissonant names like "yippies" and "hippies," these movements emerged out of the civil rights era and dissonance over the Vietnam War. Although these movements were largely centered around college campuses and populated by young white adults, they were successful in infusing some of their values to younger people. And while they did have a minimal impact on social reform, they were later co-oped by the Commercial Barons of America who used them to market every conceivable item, idea and fashion they could manufacture. What started out to be a countercultural reform movement turned into a commercial jackpot for those who were targeted by the movement. This reversal of strategy must be clearly understood lest we will continue to be deceived in regard to the dynamics which underlied this period. To put the record straight: when it became clear to these dissonant groups that America was not ready to succumb to their demands, members of these groups began to gradually compromise their positions and return to the mainstream.

The Commercial Barons realized the financial potential of their once youthful adversaries and found it in their interest to package and market the fallout which had been generated by the youth movements. The slogans and images created by these youth movements became commercialized items to be marketed and sold by the Establishment. One example of this is the commercialization of the Beatles which saturated this country in the late sixties. The Beatles had become a symbol of the new youth movement, and the Commercial Barons seized the opportunity to promote this symbol to their financial benefit. It may be debated that Black youths were not entirely seduced by this trend. This may have been true in the beginning, but due to the mass commercialization of Beatlemania, many did eventually become indoctrinated to it. Popular culture in America is not restricted to any one ethnic group for with the support of the mass media it has a way of establishing universal trends. And as I have indicated, adolescents are often the prime targets for these trends, and millions of dollars are spent annually to entice their interest. And so the Pepsi Generation Syndrome began to influence the values and lifestyles of a generation of youths who were seeking to be unique and controversial. The trademarks for this generation were the same trademarks that made GQ clothing, Christian Dior and Gloria Vanderbilt household names. In addition to these trademarks, this generation became addicted by the new electronics technology. PAC Man games, video tapes and miniature radios were consumed at rates which took even the most optimistic of the Commercial Barons by surprise. With the acquisition of these material symbols, youths adopted individualistic lifestyles and doing your "own thing" became a cherished value. Although many Black youths also adopted these symbols and values, they modified them to correspond to their lifestyles. In fact, it can be said that the pulse of America's popular culture is derived from many of the styles and expressions exemplified by Black youth which are, in turn, derived from Black folk culture vis a vis African culture. Such cultural fads as rappin', styling, hand slapping, and the various forms of popular dance can all be traced, in part, to the idioms produced by Black folk. In their in-depth study of the psychology of Black Expressions, Alfred B. Pasteur and Ivory L. Toldson make the following observation.

> Westerners are fortunate to have the examples of free expression in the black community, from which a black style has clearly derived. It is a style that now, in contemporary times, is imitated and pirated by Westerners far more frequently than it is castigated. Whatever styles Westerners enjoy in their popular arts, and in their personal lives, are borrowed, without consent of course, from the common black folk community, where the pulse of Africa is most authentically alive.[21]

The creativeness of Black youth to transform traditional modes of cultural expressions to vibrant and dynamic lifestyles is indeed remarkable. A recent example of this creativeness can be seen in "break dancing" which owes its influence to the musical antics of Chuck Berry and James Brown. However, even these two notable entertainers are indebted to African dance where forms similar to "break dancing" have been in existence before slavery, especially in Senegal.

Unfortunately, many times in the transformation of traditional modes of expression, the creators of these forms provide models which contribute little to the positive development of Black youth. In an era when Blacks are being confronted with a reemergence of overt racism and a depressed economy that compounds their chances of surviving in an oppressed environment, the models idolized by the great majority of Black youth are entertainers such as Michael Jackson, Prince, Eddie Murphy and the loquacious Mr. T. Despite their talents, these superstars only distract Black youth from identifying with lesser commercialized models whose lifestyles reflect a greater consciousness of the values that emandated from the Black cultural movement of the sixties. Consequently, many of these values have been diluted and the dilution of them is one reason many Black youth are wavering in confusion today. Many of the symbols and values which came out of the Black Cultural Movement seem to have been totally abandoned. The natural hairstyle was replaced by the Jerri Curl and "Me Pride" became a substitute for Black Pride. "Me Pride" is used in this context to describe the almost non-racial identity that some Black youths have adopted. This is not to say that they have completely disclaimed their Blackness, but rather feel it is an abstraction which has no direct influence on their lifestyles. Another way of explaining this identity confusion is to contrast the properties of "Me Pride" and "Black Pride."

ME PRIDE

Expresses self-interest and self-grafitication which ignores one's obligation to help advance the status of Black people.

BLACK PRIDE

Expresses group interest and group gratification which promotes the status of Black people.

Is an expression of African Collectivism.

The dichotomy between the two should be obvious and it should also be apparent the "Me Pride" is incongruent with the principles we advocate for the positive development of Black youths. "Me Pride" identity is completely oblivious to group affiliation and group accountability and, therefore, isolates a person from the main source (Group Identity) that distinguishes him or her from other groups. The lack of this distinction fosters misconceptions about oneself that confuses rather than clarifies a person's true identity. Black youths who are fixated to the "Me Pride" identity are less likely to understand that racism is a reaction to a collective identity which places all Black people in the same category. A Black youth who feels he or she is free of a collective identity will be deceived into believing that they will be accepted on individual merit and not judged by their group affiliation. To hold such a view in this country is not only naive but dangerous by any standard. It is a view that Lerone Bennett, Jr. describes as follows:

> In many ways, today's generation of Black youth is an enigma that bobbles the imagination. While some have benefited from the fruits of the sixties, others have wandered astray in a maze of drugs, alcohol, and psychological confusion.[22]

This latter group seems to have accepted the program white America has orchestrated for them and, as a result, their future looks indisputably bleak. In essence, however, the crisis of Black adolescence is fundamentally a reflection of the crisis that besets Black people in this country as a whole. Until Black adults make a serious effort to resolve their crisis, we can anticipate future generations of Black youths to be victimized by their own self defeating behavior and the trappings of racism.

SUMMARY OF PROBLEMS FACING BLACK ADOLESCENTS

To summarize the problems associated with Black adolescence, I have identified them as follows:

1. Adolescence in America is a traumatic experience for all youth for there are few formal structures or institutions to

give them proper direction.

2. To understand the problems of Black adolescence in America, it is necessary to view them within the context of western civilization.

3. Traditional theories regarding developmental tasks for adolescents do not take into consideration the exceptional needs of Black adolescents, and therefore, must be extended to be more relevant to them.

4. The problem of adolescence for Black youths is compounded by double standards, cultural biases and institutional racism.

5. Most Black adolescents do not receive a proper orientation to puberty which results in them developing poor attitudes about.sex.

6. Most Black adolescents are thrust into adult roles without having a meaningful adolescent experience.

7. The socialization of most Black adolescents in urban communities is molded by the Street Institution.

8. The high value once placed on the rearing of Black adolescents in the South changed dramatically when Blacks began migrating to the North in large numbers.

9. The problems associated with Black family life have placed greater stress on Black adolescents to assume adult roles.

10. Although the Pepsi Generation Syndrome was basically a reflection of the white youth movements of the sixties, it has had an impact on black adolescents.

11. Although Black adolescents are influenced by Popular Culture (via the PGS Syndrome) they try to adopt it to fit their lifestyles.

12. Many Black adolescents are addicted to the "Me Pride" identity and become confused and misguided in their values.

13. Black adolescents are targeted by white America for destruction because they represent the future and hope of Black people.

The period of adolescence for Black youths is characterized by contradictions, miseducation, ignorance, imposed adult roles, exploitation, latent self discovery and the crystallization of a value system. Indeed, it is the major crossroad that leads young people to the adult world. And the training and preparation a youth receives before making this perilous journey will largely determine if he will reach a destination filled with hope or a destination riddled by despair. But before we send our youth off on this journey, we must ask ourselves three fundamental questions.

1. What values and characteristics must future generations of Black youth possess to ensure our survival and continue our goal for liberation?

2. What will it take to harvest such generations?

3. How can we ensure that our new harvest will blossom each year so that all Black youths will have the fullest opportunity to achieve their true potential?

These are the questions this commentary will attempt to answer in the following chapters. One need not be reminded that these questions do not covet simplistic solutions or empty rhetoric. Yet a seed must be planted by someone, at sometime, somewhere, so that we can begin to examine its growth for the harvest we so badly need. I cannot guarantee that I have all the seeds to reap such a harvest. But this is not really necessary because there have always been a scattering of seeds throughout our history that have provided us with strength, direction, and purpose. Hopefully, these seeds will be rediscovered and replanted, and if new ones are found—they will only make our harvest more beautiful and more bountiful for generations yet to come.

CHAPTER FOUR

HOME IS (STILL) A DIRTY STREET
THE MYTH OF WESTERN SOCIOLOGY

> There is little reason why Negroes
> should not regard contemporary
> social science theory and
> technique with anything except
> the most unrelenting suspicion.
>
> Albert Murray
> "White Norms, Black Deviation"
> *The Death of White Sociology*

The sociology of the Black ghetcolony has received notable attention from a wide range of professional disciplines. Social scientists, anthropologists and psychologists alike have all found the study of Black people to be a compulsive topic worthy of academic and scientific research. This obsession has resulted in a voluminous number of documents, studies, dissertations and books that have all attempted to explain the social dynamics and/or problems that contribute to the Black ethos. No other racial group in America has been scrutinized so meticulously or treated as though they were guinea pigs to be analyzed in a test tube. And while the result of this rigorous examination has provided little useful information, it has all too frequently reinforced the academic diatribe discussed in the former chapters. Of all the academic disciplines, sociology and its related counterparts, has been the most flagrant conveyer of the "blame the victim" syndrome. It has been the informational incubator used to define and malign Black people.

In his review of Gunnar Myrdal's much acclaimed, *An American Dilemma*, Ralph Ellison examines the benevolent role of social science after reconstruction.

This was a period, the 1870's wherein scientific method, with its supposed objectivity and neutrality to values, was thought to be the answer to all problems. There is no better example of the confusion and opportunism springing from this false assumption than the relation of American social science to the Negro problem. And let us make no easy distinctions here between the Northern and Southern social scientists; both groups used their graphs, charts, and other paraphernalia to prove the Negro's biological, psychological, intellectual, and moral inferiority; one group to justify the South's exploitation of Negroes and the other to justify the North's refusal to do anything basic about it.[1]

Ellison then describes how whites used social science to reconcile their moral conflict regarding the "Negro Problem."

Now, the task of reconciling moralities is usually the function of religion and philosophy, of art and psycho-analysis—all of which find myth-making indispensable.

And in this, American sociological literature rivals all three: its myth-making consisting of its "scientific" justification of anti-democratic and unscientific racial attitudes and practices.[2]

Another distinguished Black writer, Albert Murray, further elaborates on Ellison's analysis.

But ill-conceived and condescending benevolence seems to be the way of American welfareism when dealing with Negroes. It is all of apiece with the exasperating convolutions of an immense number of social science theorists and survey technicians who, consciously or not, proceed on assumptions equivalent to those which underlie the rationalizations of intentional white supremacy and black subjugation. Moreover, not only are the so-called findings of most social science surveyors of Negro life almost always compatible with the allegations of the outright segregationist—that is, to those who regard Negroes as human assets so long as they are kept in subservience—they are also completely consistent with the conceptions of the technicians who regard Negroes as liabilities that must be reduced, not in accordance with any profound and compelling commitment to equal opportunities for human fulfillment but rather in the interest of domestic tranquility.[3]

In its generic sense, sociology is the study of human relationships in a particular environment(s) or as defined in the Oxford American Dictionary, "the scientific study of human society and its development and institutions, or of social problems." Like most definitions of professional disciplines, the term sociology takes on ever broader meanings, and can also be seen as being the major interpretor of a people's lifestyle, culture, and coping mechanisms. These terms place great importance on sociology and help to explain why it has such broad influence on how people are perceived.

Sociology tends to cross many professional disciplines, each possessing its own school of thought and ideological preference. This conglomerate of professional disciplines, regardless of their individual nomenclature, inevitably become the references used to define and rationalize the Black experience. And though they may appear to operate within their own professional perimeters, they invariably support each other in their analysis of Black people. For example: the social scientist perceives the Black Ghetcolony as a disorganized community; the psychologist perceives Black people as being emotionally maligned; and the anthropologist perceives Black culture in terms of so-called primitive origins. Consequently, the sociology of the Black ghetcolony usually becomes a discourse in pathology that is collaborated, in part, by diverse disciplines which all profess intellectual credibility. And of course the source of this credibility derives from its European origin whose vision is tainted by a self serving and racist interpretation of the world.

Even the founder of sociology, Auguste Comte, had a racist concept of society. Although Comte believed the sociologist must turn to ordinary historical works for his data, it was possible for him to ignore the history of non-European peoples, because, he said the sociologist is interested only in those people who have experienced social progress.[4]

It is little wonder, then, that the character of the Black ghetcolony is defined in terms which are antithetical to the interest of Black people. Youth who are constantly being told they are "underpriviledged" and "culturally deprived" will eventually identify with these nebulous terms. The Black ghetcolony child who is placed in a Headstart Program at four will become so accustomed to being labeled "underpriviledged" and "culturally deprived" that by the time he leaves the eighth grade, these words have left an indelible mark on his self image.

If we are to enhance the development of Black youth, we must consciously and systematically begin to define the character of Black people from a perspective that is truly indicative of the social and political forces which oppress us. This cannot be achieved within the context of the definitions assigned to Black people by Western sociology. It is no hidden secret that the oppressor of any people uses its intellectual status to rationalize its oppression; thereby, condoning its oppression as being either necessary and/or benevolent. To do otherwise would be to acknowledge its own inadequacies and lose its credibility in the minds of those it oppresses. So long as the oppressed accepts their oppressor's credibility or, for that matter, fails to challenge its doctrine, the oppressed remains vulnerable and dependent on their oppresors's view of the world. On the contrary, it is only when the oppressed defines their status from their view of the world will they begin to solve their problems within the context of liberating principles. By liberating principles, I mean those principles which help free a people from the intellectual diatribe used to rationalize their oppression, and which provide constructive alternatives to solving their problems.

In an earlier work, I attempted to undertake this difficult but necessary task. *Home Is A Dirty Street: The Social Oppression* of Black Children was a commentary on how social institutions fail to meet the demands of Black children, and the consequences of this failure. Specifically, it dealt with the Street Institution, the primary learning environment which prepares Black children for survival.

> The Streets of North Lawndale constitute an institution in the same way that the church, school and family are conceived as institutions. They all have a set of values and norms to govern and reinforce their existence. Of course, the social structure of the street lacks the sophistication these other institutions have. Nevertheless, it is an institution because it helps to shape and control behavior. And it is on the street where the Black child receives his basic orientation of life. The streets become his primary reference because other institutions have failed to provide him with the essential skills he needs to survive the ghetcolony; he must undergo a rigorous apprenticeship that will enable him to compensate for the lack of guidance from other institutions and adults. He becomes a student of the "asphalt jungle" because that is where he can learn the skill he needs.[5]

In addition, it discusses ths various role models which help to shape the values and life styles of Black children.

The values of the Street Institution are shaped from the physical and psychological manifestations of Black ghetcolony. From these manifestations certain life styles are created that are exemplified by the instructors of the Street Institution. The instructors consist of hustlers, pimps, street men, militants, gang leaders, and working men. And, though, these men do not have masters and Ph.D. degrees, their credentials have been earned from actual experiences and not from the sterile laboratories of formal academic institutions.[6]

The commentary was a reflection of my 16 years as a social practitioner working with Black children in North Lawndale, a ghetcolony located on Chicago's depressed west side. My introduction to this community was as follows:

Growing up in North Lawndale is more than a challenge. It is a feat that defies the manner in which children are suppose to live in this society. The very fact that they manage to endure this oppressed community is an achievement which contradicts the great odds that are stacked against them. Although they are born into a society that claims to offer a higher standard of living than any other large nation, the benefits from this prosperity fails to touch their lives. Instead, these neglected and often misguided youths receive the barest of this country's vast resources, and are dependent upon their own survival skills to cope with the oppressive elements in their environment. And despite a constant plot to destroy them, somehow most manage to survive. However, the manner in which they survive should be viewed as a travesty of American justice.[7]

The conditions and circumstances described at that time have not significantly changed as of this writing. Instead they have remained the same and some have even worsened if that is at all possible. I continued to work in North Lawndale until 1982, and if I were to write a sequel, it would be boringly repetitious. Home is (still) a dirty street for a large percentage of Black children who live in North Lawndale, and the stigmas which they wore in 1976 can still be discerned on their faces. This is not to imply that all Black children who live in North Lawndale are destined to live disrupted lives. I have seen many overcome the depressed conditions of the ghetcolony and become strong and productive men and women. But this number, important as it may be, offers little consolation when one examines the current status of many Black children in Lawndale. An examination of their status reveals the following:

—81% live in families headed by females
—50% live in families below poverty level
—47.3% live in families on public assistance
—6 out of 10 students drop/forced out of school
—North Lawndale has high incidence of crime
—Over 60% unemployment among youth
—North Lawndale is a haven for street gangs

Some people may surmise that these problems merely reflect the fallout of our depressed economy and the effects of Reagonomics. No doubt these factors have contributed, in part, to the spiraling dropout rate, rise in delinquency, increase in teenage pregnancies, and a staggering high unemployment rate. But I submit that as alarming as these factors are, it is the lack of positive programs which help make these statistics possible. And the lack of positive programs is not necessarily related to cutbacks in federal funds and Reagonomics. Positive programs do not exist in North Lawndale because most institutions that serve Black youth lack a positive philosophy which embraces liberating principles. On the contrary, these institutions are still being directed by principles which derive from the intellectual diatribe of Western sociology. As a result, they are suppose to alleviate deficiencies, instead of building upon existing strengths. And even when a few programs do emphasize strengths, they do so from a programmatic model that is deficit in design. The deficit model draws heavily from the "blame the victim" syndrome which, as I have already shown, is a product of Western sociology. Those who design social programs for Black youth persist on viewing the Black ghetcolony as an "underprivi-ledged" and "culturally deprived" community. I have rarely seen a request for proposal circulated by federal and state agencies that do not advocate the remediation of some type of deficiency. Seldom do these RFP's take into serious consideration that the majority of Black ghetcolony youth are not delinquents, drop-outs or strung out on drugs. Although the conditions for these problems exist in most ghetcolonies, it is not axiomatic that all Black youths are seduced by them. This is an important distinction to make because if we were to examine the reasons some Black youth do not become inflicted by these problems, we may discover the reasons for their immunity. And in this revelation, we can begin to identify those strengths that have enabled some Black youth to neutralize the conditions which impede their positive development. By focusing attention on these strengths, we stand a better chance of applying them to those youth who, for whatever reason, develop self defeating behavior.

In Chapter One, I listed six strengths which slave youths possessed. Of the six which were noted, the following three can be applied to our youth of today.

1. The ability to adapt to an oppressive environment without being totally debilitated by it.

2. The ability to survive with little guidance from formal institutions and a cohesive family structure.

3. The strong desire to be free.

The remaining three strengths exemplary of slave youth are not so apparent among today's Black youth.

1. A strong work orientation that allowed them to assume adult responsibilities.

2. A high regard and respect for elders.

3. An obedient attitude that enabled them to function in a cooperative manner for the general welfare of all.

It is unfortunate that the latter three strengths have deteriorated and efforts should be made to renew them. However, today's Black youth have developed two additional strengths which can be identified as follows:

1. A strong group orientation that places high value on peer relationships.

2. The resiliency to recover from setbacks and defeats.

The above strengths, when properly cultivated, can have a strong influence on the positive development of Black youth. However, for these strengths to be rekindled those who are concerned about Black youth must also have positive perceptions of them. Among these perceptions should be:

1. Black youth must be viewed in positive terms if positive programs are to be developed for them. '

2. Black youth have exceptional needs that merit bold and innovative programs.

3. Black youth are precious and should be a high priority in the Black community.

4. Black youth have the potential to be productive and responsible members of their community.

Until institutions in the Black Ghetcolony develop these perceptions, it is unlikely their programs will assist in the positive development of Black youth. But it is also improbable that these perceptions can unfold so long as institutions are molded from the intellectual diatribe of Western sociology. Among other things, sociology defines one's environment, those who populate it, and its institutions. And in this definition it makes value judgments which tend to influence the way we attempt to solve problems. When we try to solve our problems from the oppressor's vantage point, our solutions become self defeating and inimical to our self interest. To be more specific, Western sociology uses terminology that evades the real issues confronting Black people. For example, the overused term "culturally deprived" is misleading because it obscures the issue of white racism and suggests that the problem lies within the culture itself. However, when this term is translated into what it actually means, the lack of white racist culture, we are in a better position to deal with it. Western sociology is loaded with such terms, and what I'm advocating is that we begin to decipher these terms for their actual meaning and intent. Some attempts have already been made to do just this. In his discussions on an ideology of Black Social Science, Dr. Gerald McWorter presents a schematic that counteracts certain concepts which he defines as Revolutionary Pan-African Nationalist ideology. An example of these contrasting concepts is as follows:

Terms of White Social Science	Terms of Black Social Science
Negro (none-white)	African (black)
Segregation	Colonization
Tokenism	Neo-Colonialism
Integration	Liberation
Equality	Freedom
Assimilation	Africanization

Another Black social scientist, Preston Wilcox, uses a similar schematic which he calls the "rhetoric of oppression," and contrasts scientific colonialism with scientific humanism. An example of his model is as follows:

Urban Renewal	really means	Negro Removal
Model Cities	" "	Model Colonies
Human Relations	" "	Colonial Relations
Culturally Deprived	" "	Illegally Deprived
Public Welfare	" "	Public Starvation
Code Enforcement	" "	Tenant Exploitation
School Decentralization	" "	School Recentralization

While Dr. McWorther's model redefines Western terms, Mr. Wilcox's model translates them into their implicit meaning for Black people. Both models are a radical departure from the traditional way we interpret Western sociology, and as such provide an invaluable service to Black people. I do not know if either Dr. McWorter or Mr. Wilcox have expanded their models to include additional terms. And since I, too, had begun to develop similar concepts, I have prepared a glossary which deals with a more extended version of this diametrical manipulation of Western sociological jargon. I choose to use the words White Terminology and Black Translation to distinguish my model which is being presented in length.

White Terminology	Black Translation
Ghetto	Colony
Slum	Death-trap
Delinquent	Rebel
Social Welfare	Benevolent Racism

Socialization	White Indoctrination
Riot	Insurrection
Stop and Frisk	Facist Act I
No Knock	Facist Act II
Black Pathology	White Racism
Integration	White Domination
De Facto Segregation	Apartheid Act I
Ipso Facto Segregation	Apartheid Act II
Segregation	Apartheid
Lower Class	Oppressed Class
Unemployed	Exile I
Drop-Out	Exile II
Unskilled	Exile III
ADC	Paternal Racism
Prison	Concentration Camp
Jail	Compound
Inferior Education	Racist Education
Public Housing	Welfare Prison
IQ	White Ruling Norms
Social Research	Black Exploitation
Warrant	Bounty
White Liberal	Benevolent Racist
OEO	Office of Economic Oppression
HUD	Housing Unfit for Decency
Legitimate Black Leader	Neo-Colonist
Population Censor	White Surveillance
Coroner Inquest	Mocked Tribunal
Model Cities	Slum Maintenance
Head Start	Early White Indoctrination
Vagrant	Exile IV
Abandoned Building	Home for the Dispossessed
Moynihan Report	Family Instability
McCone Commission	Riot Classification Experts
Kerner Report	"I Stand Accused, So What!"
Alienation	Forced Expulsion
Citizen Participation	City Hall Controlled
Infant Mortality Rate	Genocide
Hard-Core	Exile V
Medical Center	Guinea Pig Clinic
Decentralization	Divide and Conquer
Quota System	5% Hand-picked Negroes
Patronage Job	Political Inscription

Underemployed	Victim of Economic Racism
Bootstrap Program	Reconstruction Phase II
Black Capitalism	White Controlled Economy
Law Abiding Citizen	Contented Slave
Militant	Stubborn Slave
Urban Renewal	Black De-Centralization
Poverty	Oppression
Poor People	Oppressed People
Minority Group	Oppressed Group
Community Control	White Government
Culturally Deprived	Lack of White Culture
Social Mobility	Status Quo
Civil Law	White Sanctions
Civil Rights	White Tokenism
Law Enforcement	Black Suppression
Urbanization	Colonization
Deprivation	Social Oppression
Social Norms	White Values
Poverty Program	Buffer Program
Welfare Agencies	Buffer Agencies
Social Worker	Buffer Agent
Educator	Indoctrinator
Media	Propaganda Organ
Racial Conflict	Liberation Struggle
Neighborhood Change	Emerging Colony
Open Housing	Controlled Mobility
Equal Employment	Token Job Placement
Policeman	Enforcer
Gerrymandering	Boundaries of Apartheid
Slum Clearance	Annihilation of Black People
Community Stability	Absence of Blacks
Social Adaptation	Adoption of White Norms
Civil Obedience	Conformity of White Sanctions
Cultural Ambiguity	Resistence of White Values
Power Structure	White Chauvinism
Search Warrant	Illegal Entry
Responsible Negro	Defector from the Black Black Community
Negro Leader	Puppet of White Authority
Super Nigger	Creation of White Society
Patronage System	Voluntary Slavery
Police Task Force	Gestapoe

Ward Committeeman	Plantation Boss
Street Academy	Reservoir for Exiles
Black Dialect	Bad Language
Coleman Report	Blueprint for Inferior Education
Non-verbal Child	One who uses "muthafucker"
Human Relations	White Paternalism
Job Corp	Relocation Center for Exiles
Youth Agency	Amusement Center
Under Achiever	Victim of Racist Education
Case Worker	Data Collector
Black Independence	Neo-Colonialism
American Dream	King Alfred Plan

The model I have presented differs from Dr. McWorter's and Mr. Wilcox's, but, nonetheless, retains the central principle which, I feel, each espouses. I do not view my model as being definitive and without imperfection. Hopefully, it can serve as a working model for political conscious Black social scientists to further research and develop. To illustrate how this model can be applied in screening concepts which are commonly used in Western sociology, I have taken statements from the works of a few social scientists, and translated them using the model I have presented. The italicized words constitute the key translations.

1. *White Terminology*: The *black ghettos* are overwhelmingly made up of *low-income* people, and *poverty* is the first fact of life. This has naturally encouraged the view that the *ghetto subculture* is *lower class* culture or the culture of poverty.

   Black Translation: The *Black ghetcolonies* are overwhelmingly made up of *economically exploited* people, and oppression is the first fact of life. This has naturally encouraged the view that the *ghetcolony deviant culture* is *economically exploited* culture or culture of *oppression*.

Source: Robert Blauner, "Black Culture: Myth or Reality" in Afro-American Anthropology. Norman E. Whitten, Jr. and John F. Szed (ed). New York: The Free Press, 1970, pg. 353.

2. *White Terminology*: The *social research* would seek to result in a "basic analysis" of the conditions underlying the

pathological behavior currently found in the urban public housing, and hopefully, in new proposals for social remedies for these *pathologies.*

Black Translation: The *social exploitation* would seek to result in a basic analysis of the conditions underlying the *white racist* behavior currently found in urban public housing, and hopefully, in new proposals for social`remedies for *white racism.*

Source: Lee Rainwater, *Behind Ghetto Walls*, Chicago, Aldine Publishing Co., 1970, pg. 9.

3. *White Terminology*: Public interest in *poverty* tends to focus on Negroes for good reasons. A large proportion of the *poor* are Negroes and, more important, an even larger proportion of Negroes are *poor.*

Black Translation: Public interest in *oppression* tends to focus on Negroes for good reasons. A large proportion of the *oppressed* are Negroes and, more important, an even larger proportion of Negroes are *oppressed.*

Source: David A. Schulz, *Coming Up Black: Patterns of Socialization*, New Jersey, Prentice-Hall, 1969, pg. 193.

4. White Terminology: That the *pathologic* social and physical environment of *underpriviledged* or *ghetto* children contribute to their learning disabilities is supported by ample evidence and hardly requires experimental verification.

Black Translation: That the *white racist* social and physical environment of *children who are not white* or *Ghetcolony* children contribute to their learning disabilities is supported by ample evidence and hardly requires experimental verification.

Source: Robert Friedman, "Family Roots of School Learning and Behavior Disorders," in *The Disadvantaged Child: Issues and Innovations*, Frost and Hawkes (ed) Springfield, Illionis, Charles C. Thomas, 1973.

From the above examples we can see how the translations of a few key words can alter the meaning of a concept to be more exemplary of its relationship to Black people. By redefining certain concepts, we can begin to redefine ourselves, our conditions, and our communities from our perspective. There is a major distinction between a person who lives under poverty and one who lives under oppression. While both are victims of economic exploitation, the person who lives under oppression is also a victim of political exploitation. Therefore, the manner in which both attempt to resolve their problem demands different strategies. Western social science has been used as a diversionary dogma to distract attention from America's true posture toward Black people. And in this diversion, Black people have been duped into believing its (white) mythology, and, in the process, conforming to it.

Despite the improvement in the economic status of some Blacks, over the past 10 years in particular, our ghetcolonies have literally gone unchanged. This is evident in Detroit, Newark, Cleveland, and Harlem. And it can also be seen in small hamlets like Gary, Indiana, and East St. Louis, Illinois. This commentary deals primarily with northern Black communities, for the writer has not spent sufficient time in the south to analyse conditions there. I would suspect, however, that southern cities, Atlanta, Jackson, Birmingham, and border cities like Baltimore have had similar patterns of social inertia. With little or no significant improvement in our ghetcolonies, it is naive to even think there will be improvement among our youth. Black youth are mirrors of their communities. If these communities are perceived as being pathological wastelands, many will identify with these negative properties. Conversely, if their communities are perceived as being oppressed colonies, our youth will identify with another set of properties. An underpriviledged youth will only try to cope with poverty or through perserverance escape from it. An oppressed youth understands that fundamental changes must be made in the order of society if he is to achieve his true potential. The difference between the two is merely one of perception: the underpriviledged youth seeks to become priviledged; the oppressed youth seeks to be liberated.

Home will continued to be a dirty street for millions of Black youth until we are able to help them overcome the myths of western social science, and begin to realize that they have strengths which can not only enchance their own development, but their community and race as well.

CHAPTER FIVE

"WUZ THOMAS JEFFERSON A RACIST?"
SHAPING A RELEVANT EDUCATION
FOR BLACK YOUTH

> The so-called modern education,
> with all its defects, however, does
> others so much more good than it
> does the Negro, because it has
> been worked out in conformity to
> the needs of those who have en-
> slaved and oppressed weaker
> people.
>
> Carter G. Woodson
> *Mis-Education of the Negro*

In 1983, a National Commission on Excellence in Education released a study on the status of American Public School Education that criticized the public schools for their failure to properly educate students. The study, entitled, *A Nation At Risk: The Imperative for Educational Reform*, was a major indictment against public education. In fact, its language was so incisive and it implied that the failure of the public schools to educate students threatens the very survival of America.

> If an unfriendly foreign power had attempted to impose on America the mediocre educational performance that exists today, we might well have viewed it as an act of war. As it stands, we have allowed this to happen to ourselves. We have even squandered the gains in student achievement made in the wake of the Sputnik challenge. Moreover, we have dismantled essential support systems which helped make those gains possible. We have, in effect, been committing an act of unthinking, unilateral educational disarmament.[1]

The study continues its incendiary criticism and points out the consequence of a deteriorating public school system.

> The people of the United States need to know that individuals in our society who do not possess the levels of skill, literacy, and training essential to this new era will be effectively disenfranchised, not simply from the material rewards that accompany competent performance but also from the chance to participate fully in our national life.[2]

While these caustic statements may not be a revelation to those who have been critical of public education over the years, they do reaffirm, quite poignantly, the status of millions of Black youths who are harnessed to this system. However, the study not only identifies Black youths as being victimized by this system, but reveals that white students, too, are being short changed. It is the latter revelation that no doubt compelled the Commission to be so captious of the public schools. This conclusion is made in light of the fact that public schools have historically failed Black students, but have never created such a national furor. On the contrary, when the public schools begin to fail its white students, the "nation is at risk." Despite the fact that Black students have been "at risk" for decades, it was not until white students began to suffer from education malnutrition that this nation is in jeopardy. Obviously the "at risk" status of Black students was acceptable because public education has never been responsive or accountable to their educational needs.

I do not feel I need to belabor this fact, for even the casual observer can discern the thousands of Black youths who annually become casualties of the American public schools. If anything, the Commission's study is a warning that this number will escalate; for if public education is now failing white students, the educational status of Black students must be at an all time low. Of all the institutions, excluding the family, which are crucial to the positive development of Black youths, the public school ranks at the top. We can expect little improvement among Black youths when they are continuously being denied a "decent" education. Survival in today's increasingly technological work is contingent, to a large degree, on the development of certain basic skills which are acquired through the educational process. Those who do not possess these skills will find themselves literally devoid of crucial life sustaining support systems. As a result, their chances for even a marginal subsistence are dramatically impaired. Therefore, I contend that we have little choice but to make the public schools accountable to the needs of Black youths. I'm fully cognizant of the position that some Black advocates take; that is to give up on the public schools all together. To some extent I share their position. However, when confronted by the reality that the overwhelmingly majority of Black students are dependent on the public schools for their education, I find this position to be impractical.

For most (black) Americans, quality education must be delivered through the channels of public education. Black leadership has to commit itself to the awesome task of making education a viable concept while moving simultaneously to improve the quality of life for black Americans. Such a commitment requires a confrontation with the mediocrity in the education profession and with the protectors of this mediocrity. Black leaders cannot afford to lose sight of the root cause for most of black America's ills—racism. America has a racist culture that is incapable of regulating its hostilities.[3]

Despite the development of Black independent schools and their potential for expansion, we have not yet as a people reached the level of economic commitment needed to ensure that a significant number of Black students will have access to these institutions. Education is an expensive undertaking; one which involves millions of dollars. In Chicago, for example, the school budget is nearly 90 million dollars. Even if the inordinate amount of waste that this system perpetuates is corrected, the cost would still be exorbitant. My position for focusing attention on the public schools is not to discredit the commendable record achieved by the Black independent school movement. But until the Black community makes an unilateral commitment to support this movement, the vast majority of Black students are left with little choice but to attend the public schools.

I believe this to be a fact regardless of what ideological rationale is used to support the independent school movement. The positive development of Black youths must be directed toward the nourishment of the Black masses. This will never be achieved if we ignore any segment of this precious population. To do otherwise would only contribute to the further fragmentization of the Black community. The concepts espoused in this commentary are based on the rejuvenation of all Black youths and are not intended to foster secular priorities.

I'm not suggesting that the Black Independent School Movement be ignored. On the contrary, the Black independent school can serve as a model for the public schools. Of course, I do not expect this model to be totally replicated. The fundamental philosophy of the Black Independent School is diametrically at odds with the philosophy of the public schools. Nonetheless, the Black Independent School can provide the public schools with certain principles that would not compromise its mission.

Hannibal Tirus Afrik, a tireless advocate of the Independent Black School Movement and founder of the Shule Ya Watoto in Chicago, appears to be cognizant of these principles when he identifies the IBI's relationship to the Black community.

Due to the revolutionary nature of IBIs, there is a functional relationship between them and the Black community. IBIs exists to meet the needs of the Black community by assisting in the development of community resources (social, political,

economic, religious, educational, physical, and human).
Since the community is the power base for an IBI, its
effectiveness is serving the primary criteria for its legitimi-
zation.

However, there are other roles that can best be achieved
through a consolidation of network of IBIs. These tasks
include:

1. Providing a power base for effective change in traditional
institutions.

2. Developing feasibility models of new teaching methodologies.

3. Providing opportunities to expand and apply skills
learned in traditional institutions to further develop Black
social institutions and the Black community.

4. Maintaining research information useful to Black students.

5. Providing in-service training for traditional oriented
teachers, training for new teachers, and other consultant
services.[4]

Critics of my position may argue that during the sixties
attempts were made to impact the public schools to be
accountable to the needs of Black students. True, such attempts
were made. And it is also true that most accomplished far less
than what they set out to achieve. But this was also true of other
institutions which were targeted for "institutional change."
Inspite of aggressive and sometimes revolutionary tactics, these
institutions did not yield to the wave of militancy that emerged
from a disenchanted and frustrated Black community. The
public schools became the primary target for institutional change.
In many Black communities, parents and advocates maintained
a persistent vigilance over the public schools. On rare occasions,
the public schools did bend slightly, allowing for token
community participation and Black cultural activities. But these
modest concessions did little to correct the problem of student
retardation. And when community control was sanctioned, we
learned that the public schools continued to be governed by
established institutional policies. One of the most outstanding

examples of the neocolonial character of community controlled schools was the much recorded crisis which took place at the Ocean Hill-Brownsville School in New York in 1967. With funds from the Ford Foundation, Ocean Hill-Brownsville and two other New York schools were to be showcased as prime models of community control. However, no sooner did the experiment begin when a controversy over the transfer of 19 teachers ignited a pattern of community autonomy versus bureaucratic tradition that lasted for nearly a year amid a climate of subterfuge, violence, and hostility. In the end, there was no clear victor, but there was little doubt that the students were the losers.

The infrastructure of American racism was so well fortified that it became apparent that a greater force was needed to penetrate its armour. This force was never fully mobilized in the Black community, and its struggle for "institutional change" became a ruptured dream. Notwithstanding the failures occurred during the sixties, to make the public schools accountable to the needs of Black students, we must not allow them to immobilize new efforts to deal with this problem. To assume a defeatist position that nothing can be accomplished will only ensure that Black students will continue to be denied a proper education. Granted, the strategy to change the public schools will have to be reevaluated. For instance, to rely merely on the advocacy of community residents will not in itself bring about significant change. We must also galvanize the support of Black professionals, especially from those who are employed by the public schools. To a great extent, the failure in the sixties can be attributed, in part, to this group. On numerous occasions, the struggle for control of the public schools was compounded by the actions of misdirected and self serving Black school officials. This problem still exists today as evidenced by the increased number of Black administrators in the public schools. Yet, the increase in Black administrators has not had an appreciative impact on the quality of education for Black students. I do not feel I'm being presumptious by attributing some of this dereliction to Black administrators. Black teachers must also share the blame for the failure of many Black students to achieve their academic potential. Regardless of the bureaucracy that comprise the public schools, the teacher remains the pulse of the system. When the teacher is lethargic, uncaring, and derelict, a bad system becomes even more inferior. Conversely, when a teacher shows a high self-esteem and a professional commitment to education, even the worst system will produce a significant number of competent students.

If we are to improve the educational status of Black students, we must first believe they are educable. There is sufficient evidence to show that all do not share this belief. The deficit model, mentioned in this commentary, has been so pervasive in the public school system that it has created an image of Black students which characterizes a large percentage of them as being slow learners and/or lacking in intelligence. Numerous studies have been made to support this academic diatribe. I do not intend to review these studies because I feel to do so would only acknowledge their existence, when, in fact, they should be totally ignored or better tossed in an incinerator. Black students are educable!!! Indeed, they can be taught to decipher complex math problems, analyze concepts, perform deductive reasoning, and write and speak lucidly if we have faith in their ability to learn. Even though there are social and economic factors which impact their learning abilities, nonetheless, they are educable. This is a fact which has been demonstrated in some public schools across the country. Despite the pervasiveness of institutional racism, and the debilitating effects it fosters, there are predominantly Black public schools which have been effective in educating Black students. This fact in itself should dispel the academic diatribe that Black students are not educable and serve as a challenge to all who are sincerely concerned with the education of Black youths. An example of one such school is Dunbar High School in Little Rock, Arkansas. Although this city is most noted for the integration fiasco that occurred at Little Rock High School in 1955, Dunbar High School even before that crisis developed a tradition of student achievement that continues to exist today. Despite the fact its cost per student is nearly 1/3 less than the cost per student at the predominantly white Little Rock High School, Dunbar High School has graduated over 90% of its students, many of whom have pursued higher educational goals.

Further, students were taught to set personal goals for the future. An examination of any Dunbar yearbook will show that each member of the graduating class selected a motto indicative of his/her philosophy of life and intent. Typical of such mottoes are these, selected from the 1945 Bearcat.

Always seek the highest goal in life. Be the best of whatever you are. Embrace wisdom and she shall exalt thee. Prepare today for tomorrow may be too late. He that climbs the tree of success has won the right to the fruit. It is the result of the endeavor that figures most.[5]

One of the pioneers in appraising what makes public schools effective was the late educator and researcher, Ronald Edmonds. As a member of the Harvard University faculty, Mr. Edmonds conducted numerous studies to ascertain why some schools are effective in educating Black students while others are ineffective. These studies covered schools located in oppressed communities in several major urban cities. The findings from these studies disclosed five characteristics which typify effective schools.

1. the principal's leadership and attention to the quality of instruction.

2. a pervasive and broadly understood institutional focus

3. an orderly safe climate conducive to teaching and learning

4. teacher behaviors that convey the expectation
   that all students are expected to obtain at least minimum mastery

5. the use of measures of pupil achievement as the basis for program evaluation.[6]

The above characteristics are neither revolutionary in their focus or extraordinary in their function. Yet, they comprise a set of principles which are practical and achievable if there is a willingness on the part of school administrators and teachers to properly educate Black students. Mr. Edmonds was not a pragmatist and understood that schools could be effective without all students conforming to identical levels of mastery.

To be effective a school need not bring all students to identical levels of mastery, but it must bring an equal percentage of its highest and lowest school classes to minimum mastery.[7]

I'm not suggesting that the findings from Mr. Edmonds' research are the solution to the problem of educational neglect in the Black community. However, even as guidelines for reform, they are important because they prove that Black youth are educable.

In evaluating effective schools, it has been found that among administrators, the principal plays a major role in the effectiveness of his/her school program. Other studies have produced similar conclusions. As recent as 1984, the American Associates of School of Administrators released a report that identified several functions which an effective principal provides:

1. Recruiting talented teachers and helping them grow professionally.

2. Providing instructional support through an emphasis on teaching, a positive school climate, and good resources for teachers.

3. Providing skilled supervision/evaluation of teachers.

4. Monitoring student progress closely.

5. Eliminating obstacles to the accomplishment of the school's mission.

The inferior status of the public schools in Black communities did not evolve from an unconscious plan. Quite the contrary. From a historical prospective, it represents the evolution of a racist conspiracy to keep Black people relegated to an inferior and marginal existence. Prior to reconstruction, there was no need to even conspire to provide Black youths an inferior education, because, in fact, neither the states or federal government felt Black youths should be educated. If it were not for a few missionary schools and what Carter G. Woodson called "clandestine schools" or secret schools, there would have been no educational opportunities for Black youths before this period. And to minimize these few schools, states enacted various "ignorance laws" to keep Black youths from receiving any form of education. The first of these suppressive laws was enacted in 1740 by South Carolina:

And whereas the having of slaves taught to write, or
suffering them to be employed in writing, may be attending
with great inconveniences;

Be it enacted, that all and every person and persons
whatsoever, who shall hereafter teach, or cause any slave or
slaves to be taught to write, or shall use or employ any slave
as a scribe in any manner or writing whatsoever, heereafter
taught to write; every such person or persons shall, for every
offense, forfeith the sum of one hundred pounds current
money.[8]

Although colonial America placed a high priority on
education for its "privileged whites," it did everything possible
to ensure that Blacks were denied access to this privilege.

American educational history was deeply influenced by
racism, another heritage of the nineteenth century.[9]

Even though Blacks paid school taxes, they were systematically excluded from participating in America's developing public
school system.

As a rule free Negroes paid school taxes even if their children
were not allowed to attend the schools.[10]

This exclusionary trend persisted until the Freedmen's
Bureau, created by Congress in 1865, began to provide token
supplementary funds for the education of some Blacks. But the
Black community continued to assume the major responsibility
for educating its youths; and in Philadelphia in 1833, there were
over fifty Black associations which fostered "...moral and
intellectual improvement."

Finally, as the result of Black people's relentless demands,
determination, and sacrifices, and the assistance of token
legislation, Blacks gradually began to gain access to the public
schools around 1890. Still in 1910 only 59.7 percent of Black
youths attended public schools. However, a large percentage of
these students were subjected to split shifts; denied adequate
facilities, and enjoyed few of the educational resources provided
to white students. The public school system for Black students
was not only separate and unequal, but a crude institution that
fostered miseducation and perpetuated ignorance. It was within

this maligned history that today's public schools which serve predominantly Black students were molded. If it were not for the strengths inherent to our Black youths, today's Black community would be saturated with ignorance. The point being made here is that many Black youths, over the years, have perservered a hostile school system and acquired skills to succeed in numerous professions. This should not be ignored for it could help us to examine the means by which some Black youths have emerged from the public schools without being academically paralyzed. Too often Black youths are indoctrinated by other Blacks, who have achieved some professional statue, that the public schools have little to offer them. Even though these indoctrinators are products of the public schools, they espouse this rhetoric. Surely we cannot expect our Black youths to be motivated to achieve when they are told that this is not possible within the public schools. While the public schools may never provide Black youths with a liberating education, it is fatuous to claim that they are totally irrelevant. Up to this point, I have not elaborated on the content provided Black students, but rather on their attainment of basic academic skills.

Reading, writing, and computing are still the cornerstone for a functional education. These cornerstones are imperative for Black youths even if they must be built in a hostile environment. If we do not teach them how to read, it makes little difference what the content is, anyway.

Although I have presented a dismal overview of the American public school system, I still contend we have a responsibility to make it accountable to the needs of Black youths. My contention is based on the following premises:

1. Black youths are educable;

2. There are examples of schools which are effective in educating Black youths;

3. A concentration on the strengths of Black youths can compensate, to some degree, for inferior schools;

4. Many Black youths have achieved academic competence in public schools.

What then should be the strategy to make the public schools accountable to the educational needs of Black students? Of the countless studies on public education, I have found one which I feel makes a comprehensive and plausible analysis of this much maligned system. The study was conducted by the Phi Delta Kappa Task Force on Public Education and reported in a book titled *The New Secondary Education*. Central to the study is a listing of 14 propositions which examines the flaws in secondary education and makes recommendations to correct them. Because I feel these propositions are both viable and important, they are listed in this commentary.

1. Secondary schooling as presently organized and operated does not have a powerful, beneficial, effect on learning that demonstrates it can educate adolescents with predictable results superior to other possible systems.

2. The present educational system maintains itself and resists change. Major developments in education cannot occur unless major changes are made in the system managing it. To make changes in management, one must deal with the human, historical, organizational, professional, legal, financial, and political issues involved.

3. Schooling of adolescents is often conducted in ways contradicting the nature and demands of human growth and development. Consequently, it loses power as a setting for learning. This power may be regained if schooling cultivates the student's ability to meet the tasks of personal, social and intellectual growth — the universal curriculum of human development.

4. Secondary schooling can more effectively educate students if it is more intense. It can be more intense by involving more of its constituency for more of its allotted time in educational activities which teach students what they did not previously know but can benefit from knowing.

5. Learning situations become more powerful when formal studies are combined with appropriate concrete experiences and challenging productive activities.

6. Organized and managed so that their active socializing forces contribute to learning and maturation, secondary schools will have greater influence on student achievement.

This can be done in many ways, including limiting school size and introducing more open organizational patterns to increase the range of opportunities for students to learn from adults and from each other.

7. Learning in the social domain which provides important interpersonal experiences, shared studies, and cooperative activities will enable students to relate to others better and cooperate with them more successfully. Such a program will be most effective when interactions in the secondary school and other learning situations model desirable forms of human relationships.

8. Secondary education will cultivate the gradual transition of students from childhood roles to adult roles by increasing their involvement in adult situations, issues, tasks and responsibilities.

9. Regular training and experience in selecting, designing, implementing, and managing their own learning will enable students to become independent and will prepare them for a life-time of self-education.

10. Students trained to experience and direct their own sensory, emotional, and mental functions will be better able to achieve self-understanding, self-directed learning and self-development.

11. Secondary education, in search of learning power, cannot ignore the hours adolescents spend dormant before television and other media. This time can be used for cultivating student involvement in action programs, by teaching students to relate actively to the media and by involving commercial television in the community's educational enterprise. Classroom television teaching is generally ineffective, but media resources such as video cassettes and video discs are flexible new resources for learning and teaching.

12. Secondary education will improve when the school uses the facilities, services, and personnel of the community, when the community uses the facilities, services, and personnel of the school; and when members of the community and school

system share decisions about education with equal authority and responsibility.

13. Secondary school systems can better create powerful educational experiences when they implement a process of continuous systematic program development that involves all participants.

14. New secondary school programs cannot be successfully developed and implemented without creating a supportive setting which supplies the process, organization, environments, conditions, materials, and people necessary for its success.[11]

No doubt these propositions pose a formidable task, and one cannot help but to view them with some apprehension. Though this skepticism may be merited, it should not undermine their importance. On the contrary, if we feel they are valid, they should be pursued regardless of how difficult it may be to implement them. Obviously there will be resistance on the part of the public schools to incorporate new ideas because the public schools have a history of inertia. They seem to be anchored in cement. If the Black community is to penetrate this resistance, it must engage in a massive mobilization of all of its resources. In other words, it must be able to exercise power!

Nothing has altered the only thing which white America responds to—the presence of power. If this statement sounds like a replay of the sixties, when Black Power was flaunted with unrestrained zeal, it is because the term is still valid. Regardless of its failure to bring equity to the Black community during the sixties, it remains the only force that can reverse institutional racism. This force will be realized only if we realize that it exists and commit our energies to its fruition. If the Black community is truly serious about educating its youth, it must demonstrate its commitment to collective struggle. I realized that my call for collective struggle is not a novel one. It has been echoed by many over the years. The lack of collective struggle within the Black community has been historical and an albatross on our goal for liberation. Nonetheless, it is a call that must be repeated and repeated many times over because liberation will always be only a goal until collective struggle is manifest throughout the Black community.

Black school administrators and Black teachers should assume the leadership in the collective struggle for quality education for all Black students. One vehicle for this vanguard role could be the National Alliance of Black School Educators (NABSE). Originally called the National Alliance for Black School Superintendents, when it was formed in 1971 to address the problems and concerns of this small group, its membership was expanded in 1975 to include Black teachers and other Black school personnel.

On paper, NABSE has impressive credentials. It has over 2,000 members, representing a variety of disciplines and a constitution that is strongly committed to quality education for Black students.

Purposes and Functions of the Organization

The purpose of the organization shall be to make a strong commitment to the education of all children and to black children in particular; to provide a coalition of black educators; to create a forum for the exchange of ideas and techniques; to identify and develop black professionals who will assume leadership positions in the education of black children.

The functions of the organization shall be:

Section I

To work toward the elimination of and to rectify the effects of racism in education.

Section II

To significantly raise the academic achievement level of all students and to place particular emphasis on that type of learning which builds positive and realistic self-concepts among black students.

To establish and promote the degree of awareness, professional expertise, and commitment among black educators necessary to enhance and contribute to the efforts of other educators and community persons.

Section III

To provide an avenue for recruiting school personnel in general and qualified personnel specifically.

To offer specialized training to prospective chief school officers via the development of courses for personnel through cooperative programs with institutions of higher education and school systems.

To seek to cultivate resource personnel equipped to train black educators in dealing with special problems, e.g., deficit finance, integration, student concerns, decentralization, community involvement, teacher union, etc.

Section IV
To meet and share ideas, proven programs, and guaranteed techniques for demonstrating that black youth can achieve irrespective of socioeconomic conditions.

To provide resources and intelligence banks for black school educators on proven educational programs.

To exchange information on methods of obtaining funds from federal, state, and private sources to support educational programs in the schools.

Section V
To develop positions on key educational issues which affect the education of youngsters.[12]

Obviously, NABSE must take gigantic steps to even come close to achieving these idealistic goals. In fact, it may have to start a revolution in education. As idealistic as this may appear, it is at least gratifying to see that some Black school administrators and teachers have a vision that captivates the educational needs of our Black youth. Other Black organizations which advocate the academic improvement of Black youths are the NAACP and the Urban League. Both of these traditional civil rights organizations place education high on their list of priorities. For the past seven years, the NAACP has sponsored a program called the Afro-Academic, Cultural, Technological and Scientific Olympics which encourages community support for academic achievement.

ACT-SO is designed to mobilize the black community in a massive campaign to discover and nurture black achievers in the high school classroom and award them the kind of public recognition usually restricted to the black stars of basketball and football.[13]

Local NAACP Chapters have an opportunity to participate in a national competition where winners are awarded medals plus prizes totaling $60,000. Programs such as ACT-SO are commendable because they create a climate for Black youths which reinforces their culture and motivates them to achieve. Of course the judicial arm of the NAACP has long been an advocate of quality education for Black youths. The Urban League has also used its resources to improve the quality of education for Black youths. Its most visible contribution has been as a watchdog to monitor government funds earmarked to improve schools in oppressed Black communities. This surveillance is crucial in view of the gerrymandering that often takes place to divert discretionary funds from these communities.

Another organization that offers hope for Black students is the National Coalition of Advocates for Students which was formed in 1981. NCAS is a consortium of 13 national and regional youth advocacy organizations whose goal is to assist "at risk" students in acquiring the support systems they need to achieve success in school. Its broad base makes NCSA a formidable force. Although it is an organization committed to helping students of all races, the concern for "at risk" students suggest that NCAS's largest constituency will be Black.

Black school administrators and teachers, however, must not rely solely on their membership in NABSE or other professional organizations to work in behalf of quality education for Black students. Most national organizations, despite the sincerity of their intentions, find it difficult to transform their goals to empirical realities. After their national conventions are over and the inflated rhetoric of their platform has subsided, participants go back to their communities with deflated enthusiasm. To counter this common syndrome, Black educators must become more involved in the communities where they work. The image of Black school administrators and teachers fleeing from their schools as soon as their work day ends is a common one. It appears as though many cannot bear to remain in or return to these communities exclusive of their work schedule. Granted they are often tired from interacting with students for approximately six hours each day, and should have time for their private lives and other responsibilities, nonetheless, I feel that on occasions administrators and teachers should spend additional time in the communities where they work. Even if they spend just a few additional hours each month in their communities, it would vastly improve their relations with parents and students. What I'm suggesting is merely that Black school administrators and teachers demonstrate to the communities where they work that they have more than a casual interest in the education of Black youths. Collective struggle can best be exemplified when there is a collective concern for a common cause. Black communities need to be assured that Black educators share a mutual concern in their struggle to achieve quality education. Until the image of the disconcerned Black administrator and teacher is reversed, relations between the community and Black educators will continue to be strained. Such relations will never foster the type of collective effort that is essential to developing and maintaining quality schools for Black youths.

Although the Black school administrator should be the major catalyst for improving these relations, the Black teacher is in the best position to impact students. Of all the adult models which Black youths are exposed to, the Black teacher can become the most influential—that is if the teacher realizes this potential and uses it judiciously. Some of the characterizes of an effective teacher are:

1. Someone the students can look upon as an instrument of behavior change.
2. Someone they can harken to, to listen to, and someone who provides incentives of motivation.
3. Someone they can look upon as a symbol of new life.
4. Someone they can relate to, and he/she listens.
5. Someone who thinks the students are individuals, not merely a stereotyped group.
6. Someone that a large portion of students would like to have as a friend.

7. Someone who is out to help the students and not as a demogogue.

8. Someone devoted to his job and humanism.

9. Someone sympathetic to the needs of his students.

10. Someone students can take into confidence.[14]

If Black school teachers are to reflect these characteristics, they must possess a high self esteem and belief that all Black youths are educable and deserving of a quality education. I cannot over-emphasize the importance of these qualities because they are fundamental to student motivation and student responsiveness. In my experiences with teachers (Blacks included) I have found many to be unfit to teach Black students. Because of their personal hang-ups and personal agendas, these teachers only contribute to the chronic ineffectiveness of most public schools. In *Home Is A Dirty Street*, I attempted to characterize the types of teachers who generally teach Black students:

1. **Benevolent Misfit** — allows benevolent attitude toward Black students to compensate for inability to teach them.

2. **Frustrated Cynic** — is repulsed by having to teach Black students and constantly complains about the school system but does nothing to improve it.

3. **Confirmed Racist** — hates Black students.

4. **Social Technician** — uses Black students as guinea pigs to reinforce deficit concepts.

5. **Bureaucratic Freak** — is addicted to regulations and has no flexibility.

6. **Social Advocate** — believes Black students can achieve and works diligently to provide them with a quality education.[15]

Since identifying the above types, I would now add two more to this list:

7. **Chronic Apologist** — makes excuses for everything that goes wrong in the classroom.

8. **Accommodationist** — is willing to go along with any policy regardless of its effect on Black students.

Of the above types, only the Social Advocate possesses the disposition to properly teach Black students. Unfortunately this type is rare and consequently the majority of teachers who teach Black students have little concern for their educational development. It is not accidental that most Black students receive poor instruction in the classroom. Yet the classroom sets the tempo which determines how they respond to the educational process. When this tempo is orchestrated by chaotic teaching it only induces negative vibrations which are internalized by the students. The students, in turn, respond accordingly and the end result produces an environment that is not conducive to either teaching or learning.

This commentary is not suggesting that teaching Black students is a simple task. Quite the contrary, it demands considerable tolerance, patience, flexibility, creativity, professional skill and above all a genuine concern for their well being. Youths who are products of an oppressive society should not be expected to be free of hostile attitudes, misguided values and disruptive behavior. The very nature of their survival instincts often make them overract to authority and regulated constraints. But these conditions do not mean Black youths cannot learn, only that the manner in which they are taught should be adapted to their exceptional needs. When these exceptional needs are ignored, teachers will most likely continue to use dysfunctional teaching practices. The failure to acknowledge this problem compounds the already arduous task inherent to the process of traditional teaching.

Of course a strong case can be made in behalf of teachers in defense of their poor attitudes and ineffectivenss. There is a consensus among most that they are underpaid for the important work they perform. As the result many feel they are not appreciated and have no motivation to do anything beyond the minimal teaching requirements. This attitude may not mirror the "protestant work ethic," but in an era of high inflation, status seeking and self serving values, it should be understood, if not accepted. I do concur that teachers are underpaid. Although I question whether increased salaries will necessarily produce effective teachers; nonetheless, their salaries should be commensurate with their responsibilities. And their responsibilities are enormous. Few professions, if any, can match the responsibilities assigned to teachers. The education of its young should be a nation's highest priority and those who are responsible for teaching should be adequately compensated. Some school systems have begun to acknowledge this fact and have initiated incentive programs for effective teachers. Those who oppose these programs feel they rely too heavily on subjective data which may not fairly measure a teacher's performance. Advocates of this movement feel that although these incentives may not be free of bias, it is an effort to award those teachers who are more effective in the classroom. I feel if incentive programs can demonstrate even a slight improvement in the performance of Black students that they should be implemented. It should be apparent that something must be done to alter·those traditions which have long proven to be unsuccessful. The standards I recommend for Black educators are high and will not be easy to achieve. But the cost of having another generation of uneducated and miseducated Black youths will be even higher. Black educators cannot defer their commitment to provide quality education to Black youths any longer.

I have deliberately separated the need to ensure all Black youths develop basic skills from their need to have an education that incorporates liberating principles. My reason for the separation is because I feel Black youths must first have these skills before they can begin to conceptualize these principles. Then, too, I have strong doubts as to whether the public schools can ever be revolutionized to provide Black youths with a liberating education. Paulo Freire confirms my skepticism in his revolutionary analysis of oppressed people when he concludes:

> It would be a contradiction in terms if the oppressors not only defended but actually implemented a liberating education.[16]

Although Mr. Freire's thesis deals primarily with the oppressive conditions of the people who live in the North East of Brazil, there are parallels in his analysis which are applicable to our oppression in America.

Reality which becomes oppressive results in the contra-distinction of men as oppressors and oppressed. The latter, whose task it is to struggle for their liberation together with those who show true solidarity, must acquire a critical awareness of oppression through the praxis of this struggle. One of the gravest obstacles to the achievement of liberation is that oppressive reality absorbs those within it and thereby acts to submerge men's consciousness.[17]

When Mr. Freire speaks of acquiring "a critical awareness of oppression" and why "oppressive reality . . . acts to submerge men's consciousness," he is also describing the thesis of Carter G. Woodson's landmark book, *The Miseducation of the Negro:*

The same educational process which inspires and stimulates the oppressor with the thought that he is everything and has accomplished everything worthwhile, depresses and crushes at the same time the spark of genius in the Negro by making him feel that his race does not amount to much and never will measure up to the standards of other people. The Negro thus educated is a hopeless liability of the race.[18]

Carter G. Woodson succinctly describes how public education has been used to control the minds of Black students. Mr. Woodson placed little value on this type of indoctrination because it failed to educate Black students to confront their oppressors.

The only question which concerns us here is whether these 'educated' persons are actually equipped to face the ordeal before them or unconsciously contribute to their own undoing by perpetuating the regime of the oppressor.[19]

Black students are mis-educated because it is not in the interest of white America to have them know the truth about how they have been systematically denied access to the so-called American Dream. The mechanism used by white America to facilitate this pattern is through institutional racism, of which the public school is a prime conveyor. This accounts for the reason, if one assumes the supposition that not all school administrators and teachers are racists, the system is still able to implement its racist dogma.

Institutional racism is the action taken by a social system or institution which results in negative outcomes for members of a certain group or groups. An institution or social system, which is defined as any procedure or set of procedures that is regularly undertaken to accomplish some implicit or explicit purpose, can vary from table manners to the manner in which agencies of the federal government are run. Most people tend to think of their behavior, particularly in race relations, as an individual, one-to-one proposition. Thus, if a white has not done something bad to a black recently, there is supposedly no racism; but institutions tend to dominate and control the lives of most people much more than they realize.[20]

As a result, even when Black youths acquire basic cognitive skills, they generally have a vision of the world that is pro-white and anti-Black. Consequently, if Black youths are to be properly educated they must not only know that the correct spelling of "was" is W A S and not W U Z but be taught the truth about their history and those who have maligned it. For example, the public school prescribes an education based on the philosophy and ideals espoused by the shapers of the American Constitution. Within this philosophy, America is portrayed as a democratic society that ensures equal justice to everyone and men like George Washington and Thomas Jefferson are canonized as national heroes. Yet when this philosophy was formed, Blacks were in slavery and George Washington and Thomas Jefferson were proponents of this dehumanizing system. Both were "heralded men" who owned slaves at one time in their lives. Even though Blacks had fought valiantly against the British at the onset of the American Revolution, slaves were forbidden to enlist when Washington assumed command of the American army. It was not until after the slaughter of American troops at Fort Valley in 1777 did Washington rescind this order because he was in desperate need for more men. And although the "humanitarian" Thomas Jefferson chastised the King of England for perpetuating slavery in a clause which was removed from the final draft of the Declaration of Independence, he later approved the signing of the Missouri Compromise which sanctioned slavery south of the Mason Dixon. Then, too, his passionate rhetoric of "equality for all men" could not atone for his ownership of slaves. In fact, Thomas Jefferson was alleged to have had a slave mistress named Sally Hemings who gave birth to five of his children. Lerone Bennett, Jr. makes the following statement about this "alleged" affair.

It was widely said and believed in the slave period that Jefferson had slave mistresses and slave children. His favorite mistress, the reports said, was 'Black Sal.' Fair-skinned with long hair and Caucasian features, Sally Hemings played an important role in several political campaigns.[21]

Mr. Bennett further mentions the findings of Pearl M. Graham, a scholar who has researched the lineage of Thomas Jefferson's family.

From a study of contemporary and modern sources, Miss Graham has proven, to her satisfaction anyway, that Sally Hemings bore Jefferson 'at least four children, possibly six.' The children as listed by Jefferson under the name of Sally Hemings in his Farm Book were:

Hemings, Sally, 1773
   Beverly, 1778
   Harnet, May, 1801
   Madison, Jan., 1805
   Eston, May, 1808[22]

Jefferson's position on slavery remained subject to interpretation throughout his life, and he could not purge his infamous role as a slave master from the annals of history.

I have used this example of the contradictions fashioned by Thomas Jefferson to illustrate why Black youths need to have a critical awareness of Western history and develop a level of consciousness that is cognizant of and supportive of our struggle for liberation. Although armed struggle may be the most dramatic force used by oppressed people to free themselves from oppression, the mind must, first, be perceptive enough to engage in meaningful struggle. When Black youths' awareness is clouded with ignorance and misconceptions, they will be at a disadvantage if, in fact, they choose to engage in this serious task. The system of oppression in America is veiled with benevolency, paradoxes, neo-slavery, tokenism, and patronizing rhetoric that hides its true identity. Because of this camouflaged image, it is not always easy to expose its culprits and decipher its contradictions. Only when Black youths are able to decodify its aberrations will they be able to confront their oppressors in a non-reactionary and constructive way. A liberating education would provide Black youths with an awareness to screen out these aberrations and prepare them to serve in the best interest of the Black community. This is not an appeal to incite Black youths to engage in armed struggle, but a rationale for why they need an education that helps them to shed the oppressive fabric which stifles and retards their intellectual development. A liberating education for Black youths must, thus, provide the following:

1. an awareness and appreciation of their racial and cultural heritage;

2. an understanding of all forms of racism;

3. an understanding of colonialism, neo-colonialism, plantation politics, neo-slavery, and uncle Tomism;

4. an understanding of their kinship with other people of African descent throughout the Black Diaspora;

5. an understanding of how and why the system of capitalism works in favor of the ruling class;

6. an understanding of the contradictions and hypocrisy in American democracy;

7. an understanding of social class and racial division;

8. the ability to distinguish who is their friend and who is their enemy;

9. an understanding of the trappings of popular (western) culture, and how it serves as a diversion to positive Black life styles and values;

10. an understanding of western social theory and how it is used to stigmatize and depreciate Black people;

11. how to establish goals which are supportive and consistent with the needs of Black people;

12. an understanding of their roles as the future leaders and cornerstones for the Black race;

13. an appreciation of the humanness of Black people.

The list which I have mentioned is not intended to be complete and absolute. The systemic nature of American oppression is multi-faceted and crosses every conceivable economic, cultural, political, and educational institution. Indeed, it saturates the "American way of life." Nonetheless, a true liberating education for Black youths must take all these things into consideration if, in fact, they are to successfully combat the pervasive presence of American and Western oppression. This is a tall order, perhaps even an overly indealistic one. But this commentary was not written to preserve the status quo. It was written to harvest a future generation of Black youths who will be free of self-defeating behavior and attitudes, and who will respond to the liberating needs of Black people.

Contrary to the belief held by some critics of this type of education, there are a few models which speak to this agenda. Because of the strong attraction and, yes, belief in the present educational system, many of us fail to explore other alternatives for Black youths. Yet these alternatives do exist if only we would remove our blindfolds and look for them. For example, the Council of Independent Black Institutions has developed a culture-based curriculum for Black youths that incorporates many of the items I have listed. This curriculum spans the pre-school to secondary level. The Black Child Development Institute, Inc. is another organization which has responded to this task. I would also include the Cultural Linguistic Model developed at the Department of Inner City Studies at Northeastern University in Chicago. This model uses the language of Black youths as a legitimate learning device to facilitate their appreciation of Black culture, and has been used in public schools in Kansas, Ohio, California, and Illinois. Another important source which deserves mention is the *An Afrocentric Educational Manual* prepared by Ms. Jualynne E. Dodson of the Atlantic University School of Social Work. This manual is primarily designed to be used in workshops for orienting teachers to non-deficit concepts for developing effective programs for Black youths and their families. I would also recommend *A Non-Racist Framework for the Analysis of Educational Programs for Black Children* which focuses on the Black community as being the primary molder of Black youths. No doubt there are other models which expressively address the liberating needs of Black youths.

The question remains ... who will expand and implement these models? Because of my perception of the public schools, I feel it's not logical to think they will ever undertake this task. We should not expect the public schools to abolish its racist philosophy to placate to the liberating needs of Black youths. While I do advocate we should expect and demand the public schools to teach Black youths basic cognitive skills, I harbor no illusions about them providing our youths with a liberating education. We have already betrayed our youths in allowing them to believe in this idiotic thinking—that their oppressor will also free them from the shackles of mental slavery. But these shackles remain despite our faith in integration, desegregation, equal opportunity, and other civil rights legislation. The same system that allowed Kunta Kinte and millions of other African youths to be branded by slavery remains in tact. It has merely modified its methods, but has not abrogated its goal.

The responsibility for this task must be assumed by the Black community. To complement the laudable efforts of the independent black institutions, other Black institutions must show a greater accountability to the educational needs of Black youth. In particular, the Black church must respond to this challenge. Though it has been able to erect new buildings for worship, it has been derelict in using these structures for educational purposes as was the case in the nineteenth century when Black people were completely locked out of white institutions and depended solely on their churches for their educational needs. In addition, the many Black Greek organizations, lodges, and various social groups should employ their resources to meet this challenge. As difficult as this task may be, it is not beyond the resources indigenous to the Black community. The catalyst for mobilizing these resources is called commitment. This commitment can be activated with a renewed faith in Black youths and the unyielding belief that they are the seeds which will one day yield a harvest for a new generation of liberated Black men and women.

PEDAGOGICAL SCHEMATIC FOR THE POSITIVE
EDUCATION OF BLACK YOUTH

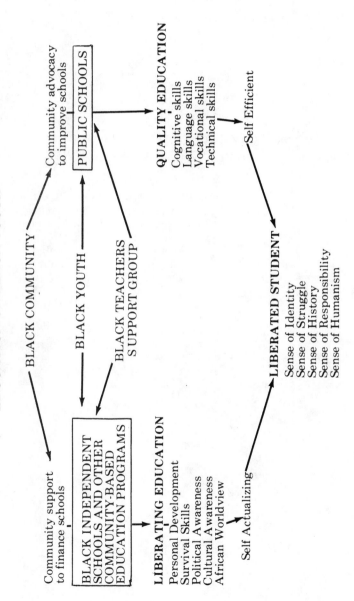

Useni Eugene Perkins
Copyright © 1985

CHAPTER SIX

DO BOYS BLEED TOO?
THE CRISIS IN TEENAGE PREGNANCY

> Despite better sex education and
> better methods of birth control,
> pregnancy among Black teenagers
> has reached staggering propor-
> tions and threatens not only the
> future of our children but the
> very survival of the Black race.
>
> Louise Meriwether

Judy Brown found it difficult to control her anxiety as she entered the small kitchen of the three room Harlem flat she shared with her 33 year-old mother and two younger sisters. Her well developed breasts made her look much older than her thirteen years. However, a close examination of her adolescent features quickly negated such a premature appraisal. Judy appeared sullen as she strained to get her mother's attention who was busy preparing a pot of collard greens. Ms. Brown finally sensed Judy's presence and stopped her culinary chores.

"Wat's wrong, child? You look like you done lost your best friend."

Judy tries to disguise her anxiety. "No, I ain't lost my best friend."

"Well wipe that sad look off your face, child, I got enough troubles without having to deal with yours, too!"

"I don't mean to worry you none, ma dear. It's just that..."

"Well, what is it? The Lawd didn't give you that mouth just to stuff it with food. Now, what's bothering you, child?"

Judy begins to fondle her breast.

"I haven't been feeling well lately, ma dear. And my er—tits are real sore."

Her mother begins to show more concern. That's because you're growin' up. They won't be sore all the time. Just don't press on them too much. And...I suppose I got to get you a larger bra."

Judy continues to sulk. "But there's something else I gotta tell you, ma dear."

"Yes!"

"Well...I also been having cramps...and..."

"Go on with it!"

By this time Judy can no longer hold back her tears and begins to cry. "I also threw up this morning."

Ms. Brown begins to suspect what the problem is. "When did you have your period last?"

Judy wipes her eyes and begins to contemplate. "I . . . er think it was about three months ago."

"You mean you ain't had a period in three months. I'll be damn, child. You must be pregnant!"

The scene which I have described has become all too common in the Black community. It is a scene that has raised considerable concern among social workers, educators, and, of course, the parents of the thousands of Black "girls" who are annually helping to swell the national census of Black America. The rash of pregnancies by Black teenage girls, though they have decreased slightly in recent years, constitute a most serious problem. The phrase "babies having babies" aptly describes the social epidemic which has escalated to such proportions that nearly six out of every ten births in the Black community are delivered by a teenager. Other statistics reveal the following:

— Eighty three percent of births to Black teens occur outside of marriage;

— 6.6 percent of Black teenagers who are pregnant have abortions;

— The infant death risk is 30-300 percent higher for teenage mothers than for mothers in their 20s.

— Maternal mortality is also considerably higher for teenage mothers, especially among young adolescents;

— Girls aged 10-14 years of age have a higher rate of post-neonatal death and two times higher rate of fetal death than women in their 20s.

— Teenage mothers are far more likely to have babies that are premature or of low birth weight (less than 5.5 pounds).

— Low birth weight is a major cause of infant mortality as well as a host of serious childhood illnesses, birth injuries, and neurological defects, including mental retardation and developmental disabilities.

To compound these health and medical problems which often accompany teenage pregnancies, there are also grave social implications:

—Black women who bear children during their teens are more likely to be permanently victimized by what has been called "The feminization of poverty."

—The number of black teenager youths who annually drop out of school due to pregnancy is approximately 45,000.

—48 percent of all mothers who had their first child before the age 18 do not receive a high school diploma.

—Black unwed fathers are less likely to complete their education and have greater difficulty gaining employment.

—Children of teenage mothers are more likely to remain in poverty.

—Children of teenage mothers are more likely to experience problems in school.

—Children of teenage mothers are high risk for child abuse and child neglect.

—Teenage parents are a high risk for drug abuse and alcohol abuse.

—Most teenage mothers will have subsequent pregnancies while still in their teens.

Although the problem of Black teenage pregnancy has persisted since the late 50s, it was not until the mid 70s that it became a major concern among a significant number of Blacks. One reason for this belated concern was probably due to the belief held by some Blacks during the 60s that the procreation of babies was an intrinsic part of the Black liberation struggle. Those who held this belief also believed that any effort to curb the birth rate of Black babies was an act of genocide.

In her detailed and brilliant study of Black girls growing up in the Pruitt-Igoe Housing Complex in St. Louis, Missouri, Dr. Joyce Ladner comments on this attitude:

> Militant and revolutionary Blacks argue that the dispensation of contraceptives through public health clinics and private agencies such as Planned Parenthood is a genocidal tool that is designed to decrease the Black population.[1]

As a result of such arguments, programs which emphasized family planning, birth control, and sex education were con-

demned as being counter revolution to Black people. Unfortunately, these beliefs were not vigorously challenged, and their
promoters took pride in eliciting chauvinistic and irresponsible
rhetoric. Child bearing to these advocates was seen as a political
obligation, but they failed to weigh the consequences of its
social ramifications. Toni Cade describes her reactions after
attending a (revolutionary) meeting where brothers were
promoting child bearing as the foundation for "nation building."

> Since then I've been made aware of the national call to the
> Sisters to abandon birth controls, to not cooperate with an
> enemy all too determined to solve his problems with the
> bomb, the gun, the pill; to instruct the welfare mamas to
> resist the sterilization plan that has become ruthless policy
> for a great many state agencies; to picket family-planning
> centers and abortion referral groups and to raise revolu-
> tionaries.[2]

Even among informed Black social scientists, the problem
of teenage pregnancies was reduced to whispers. One of the
phenomenon of social oppression is that the oppressed often
conceals or denies the gravity of a problem when that problem
has been identified by their oppressor. This is done so as not to
give their oppressor a sense of "being correct" even when the
oppressor "is correct" in identifying a problem. During the 60s,
white social scientists were quite vocal about the rise in teenage
pregnancies largely because white girls were leading this
escalation. However, the seriousness of the problem in the
Black community was conveniently ignored or rationalized as a
"non-problem." As a result, the Black teenage pregnancy
problem became lost in a maze of disconcern, racial pride, and
political bickering.

Although there may not be a significant correlation between
the rise in Black teenage pregnancies and the posturing of some
Blacks to promote child births during the midfifties, I feel the
two factors did have an implicit cause and effect relationship.
I'm not suggesting that the pro childbirth advocates can be
blamed for the rise in Black teenage pregnancies. The social
factors which ignited this trend were no doubt complex,

culturally rooted and most likely void of politics. Nonetheless, the pro-childbirth advocates did have an impact on programs which were designed to curb teen pregnancies. Pro-childbirth advocates were successful in mounting opposition to these programs and limiting their implementation in the Black community.

In retrospect, however, I cannot really claim that the support of these programs by the pro-childbirth advocates would have caused a significant decrease in Black teenage pregnancies. On the other hand, I can surmise that their support of these programs would have raised community awareness about the seriousness of the rising birth rate among Black teenage girls. It was this lack of awareness that was largely responsible for the failure of the Black community to collectively address this problem.

Today, most Blacks will agree that the trend of Black teenagers having babies in the mid-fifties has had an adverse impact of the Black community.

Teenage pregnancy is one of the major problems confronting the Black community today. At risk is the healthy development of a new crop of children. More than any other group, Black teen mothers lack the necessary resources to adequately care for their offspring.[3]

Unless we are able to offer these young parents the crucial support systems needed to raise children and provide assurances that their children will have an opportunity to achieve their potential, we must do something immediately to halt this crisis! To allow this trend to continue without these resources will only add to an already spiraling number of poorly supervised Black teenagers who will enter the 21st century with social handicaps which will most likely main them for the remainder of their lives. Throughout this commentary emphasis has been focused on the positive development of Black youth. However, this call cannot be answered if we continue to allow young girls to have babies, *babies* who will have little chance to even begin to respond to the challenges which confront our future generations. It is difficult enough for youth who are the offspring of "mature" adults to meet this challenge to believe that the offspring of "immature" children can successfully achieve this goal. Dr. Frances Cress Welsing, a child psychiatrist and pediatrician and an outspoken critic of Black teenage pregnancy shares this perception:

> There is no teenage child, male or female who is able to consistently carry out this function—this task of shaping and molding a human being. It takes maturity to teach maturity. Children can only teach children to behave as children. It requires emotional maturity to withstand the stress of racism as it is manifested in the multiple areas of life activity: economics, education, labor, law, politics, and war. Children are unable to teach how to withstand this stress system.[4]

Dr. Welsing also views this problem as a clear and present danger for the Black community.

> In brief, it is impossible to have a healthy Black community in the presence of the immature and inadequate parenting of Black children.[5]

To compound the problem of "babies having babies," there is the economic factor that makes raising children today a formidable task. According to a National Urban Institute study, it takes $142,000 to adequately raise a child from birth to age eighteen. Although this figure is undoubtedly scaled for white middle class children, even a third of it presents an economic strain on most Black parents.

Aside from the fact that few teenage girls are mature enough and have the necessary resources to adequately raise children, there is also a recurring theme which I feel stigmatizes Black teenage pregnancies. This theme was first conjured during slavery when the main function of a Black female was to bear children. This function was believed to be their only value and it was further denigrated by the slavemaster's licentious perception of Black women.

As manufactured sex objects, female slaves were exploited at will by whites and many even defiled by Black studs who functioned as sex predators. This latter function has survived slavery and may account for one reason many young Black males show little respect for the virtues of Black femininity. These young Black males have been indoctrinated with the image of the oversexed, promiscuous, exotic women and take pride in "making it with a sister."

Black males, for instances, have had a strong sexual orientation because the sexual conquest of women was considered a masculine trait. Since other symbols of masculinity have been denied in the society, sexual prowess became a partial substitute in other areas. Thus, the black male who has a variety of pre-marital sexual experiences occupies a prestigious position in his peer group.[6]

The sister, in turn, may also be indoctrinated with the same image, and responds to the sexual advances without opposition. Dr. Joyce A. Ladner provides an explanation for these perceptions.

Many of the conventional codes regarding pre-marital sex have little significance for the girl growing up in the Black community. The low-income Black community has always been stereotyped as having "loose morals" and "promiscuous" behavior in the area of sex.[7]

However, Dr. Ladner also makes a distinction between middle class sex values and values of low-income Black people which are often diametrically at odds with each other.

What is not taken into consideration in these assertions is that a different set of moral codes regulates the sexual behavior of Black people...Thus pre-marital sex is not regarded as an immoral act. It is viewed as one of those human functions that one engages in because of its natural functions.[8]

Assuming Dr. Ladner's analysis is correct—that premarital sex in the Black community is often perceived as a human function of adolescents, it is little wonder teenage pregnancies have become a serious problem in light of the studies which have shown that teens are more sexually active today than in any time in the past. But studies have also shown that the majority of teenage pregnancies are the result of steady dating and not casual relationships. Dr. John Porter makes the following observation about the options associated with "romantic dating."

> For the young, romantic love for all of its lighthearted illusions serves several constructive purposes. Dating serves the romantic love notion of extending or postponing unrestrained sexual intercourse until marriage ... Through the romantic interlude of dating, a couple wishing to postpone sex until after marriage can short circuit sexual consummation by showering each other with tenderness and imaginative longing.[9]

However, Dr. Porter also acknowledges that romantic relationships without sex can pose emotional problems.

> This isn't easy for many couples, especially males who plead that "I can't hold out much longer." Some couples succumb to pre-marital sex. Often, a girl fears that if she doesn't give in, she may lose her man to another girl who "will do it."[10]

Black teenage girls have been the subject of few studies and, consequently, when we attempt to analyze the Black teenage pregnancy problem, we tend to rely on conjecture, myths, and undocumented data. The importance of Dr. Ladner's study, among its other contributions, is that it fills this void and provides us with empirical data about the attitudes and beliefs of Black girls toward pre-marital sex and pregnancy. An extrapolation of some of these attitudes and beliefs cited in Dr. Ladner's study reveal the following:

— Black girls generally have two opposing attitudes toward pre-marital sex:
  1. to engage in sexual relations and accept whatever consequences might follow or
  2. to abstain from pre-marital sex.

— Black girls generally feel that having the first child out of wedlock is a mistake which a girl is entitled to make. However, they feel that having a second child out of wedlock is an indication of a girl's promiscuity and immorality.

— Although Black girls are ambivalent about the birth of children out of wedlock, they normally do not weigh this act in terms of morality versus immorality, but "within the context of economic realities."

—Regardless of the factors that may cause a girl to have a child out of wedlock, most Black girls believe the child should not be stigmatized.

—Black girls generally feel that children born out of wedlock should not be surrendered to adoption agencies, but remain in the custody of the mother, grandparents, or another member of the girl's extended family.

—Most Black girls who become pregnant would like to have the security of marriage but not under conditions which they feel are incompatible to them.

—Most Black girls are willing to accept the responsibility of rearing their children even though they realize they lack the emotional maturity to do so.[11]

From the above data, we can discern that Black girls have attitudes and beliefs about pre-marital sex and pregnancy which sharply differ from those attitudes and beliefs sanctioned by the white middle class (and some Blacks as well). Because of these differences, it should be apparent that conventional methods for dealing with teenage pregnancy will not meet the unique needs of Black girls. Instead, we must approach the problem of Black teenage pregnancy in terms of its relationship to the cultural traditions and norms which have helped to insulate the Black community from being totally debilitated by racism and oppression.

While Dr. Ladner's study provides a balanced and well documented commentary on the socialization of low-income Black girls, it does not explain the reason(s) for the boom in Black teenage pregnancies during the mid-fifties. Assuming that Dr. Ladner's findings reflect the cultural traditions of a particular Black community that can also be identified with other Black communities, the question of why Black teenage pregnancies did not pose a serious problem in the past becomes germane. This question is relevant because the answer(s) may provide directions for dealing more effectively with the problem today. If, as I have assumed, our cultural traditions are the determinants for our behavior, then we must ask: what changes . . . have taken place in these traditions to influence the sharp difference in the sex behavior of Black teenagers today as compared to yesterday?

In an attempt to respond to this question, I have identified a list of factors which I feel contributed to the rise in Black teenage pregnancy during the mid-fifties.

1. The overall climate in sexuality and sex relationships in America after World War II was more promiscuous and free of previously held sexual taboos and sexual morals which were recognized, in part, by all ethnic groups.

2. The Women Liberation Movement which brought greater attention to the sexual independence of women in most aspects of their lives.

3. The various counter-cultures that emerged in the mid-fifties, i.e., hippies, yippies, flower children, etc., were more sexually oriented and overt in their attitudes toward sex.

4. The increasing freedom of the media, especially the movie industry, to be more explicit in their portrayal of sex. This would also include magazines such as Playboy and its counterparts.

5. An increase in the Black youth population as the result of the "baby boom" during World War II. According to the Bureau of the Census study Black Population in the United States: An Historical View, 1970-1978, the Black youth population rose from 30 percent in 1940 to 37 percent in 1960. This figure is relevant because an increase in the number of Black youths would also raise their chances of having more babies — especially in light of the previous factors which I have listed.

6. A decline in Black two parent households after 1940 which according to the same report dropped from 77% to 68% in 1970. Today this percentage is close to 54%. This figure is relevant because it strongly suggests that family disciplines are more likely to weaken when one parent is absent. It would also appear logical that the monitoring of sex habits and attitudes would be affected by the break down in family discipline.

7. The stigma of a girl having a baby in the Black community became less binding and young mothers were no longer ostracized by their peers.

8. The increasingly number of frustrated and alienated Black youth who began to establish their own set of values to govern their behavior.

9. The rising popularity among many Black female teens to have their own children.

10. The earliest physical and biological maturing of the vital sex organs among youth of all ethnic groups which are necessary for pregnancy.

11. Youth of all ethnic groups have simply become more sexually active.

12. Black teenage girls are less likely to use contraceptives or have abortions.

The list I have developed is not intended to be conclusive or immune from criticism. It is merely a frame of reference to help us better understand the social and physical dynamics which were most likely prominent in influencing the rise in Black teenage pregnancies during the mid-fifties. If I were to list one problem, above all the rest, that will do more harm to the positive development of Black youth, I would unequivocally identify teenage pregnancy. Socialization starts at birth, and when a child begins his/her life in an environment that is void of proper pre-natal care, mature parenting and crucial life support systems, it is highly improbable that that child will accumulate the types of experiences which will enhance his/her maturity during adolescence. Although I have indicated in Chapter 3 that the childhood and pre-adolescent years do not always constitute a permanent mold for future behavior, the adolescent years are made easier when the former two (childhood and pre-adolescence) have less problems and greater stability. Children of teenage parents are destined to have greater difficulty in realizing their potential. This is particularly true of those children whose parents are also poor, oppressed and Black.

The consequences of early births for Black female teens are

well documented and provide a grim picture for both mother and child. However, lost in this ominous picture is the status of the teenage father. Yet, when one closely examines the problems associated with Black teenage fathers, they are equally distressing and severe. In a study conducted by Dr. Leo E. Hendricks of 20 unwed adolescent Black fathers, some of these problems were articulated in the following table:

Table 2

In your opinion and from what you have seen yourself, what are some of the problems you have faced as a young father?

A Representative Range of Problems
Faced by Young Fathers

"Providing financial support to the mother of my two children."

"Sometimes misunderstanding with Mother (i.e., unwed mother) about various things."

"Disadvantage to be young and try to raise kid in proper way."

"She wants to marry before I finish school and I want to wait until I get myself straight."

"Problems with her (i.e., unwed mother) father."

"Money problems."

"Not being able to buy clothes for the baby."

"Finding a good nursery to take care of child."

"Marriage."

"Girl's mother resented me."

"Not being able to support the baby myself."

"Mother of girl (i.e., unwed mother) get in the way."

"Can't see the baby when I want to."

"Payment of bills."

"Not being able to go to school."

"None."*

---

*Four (4) of the fathers gave this response.[12]

Of course one has to be extremely careful in arriving at a conclusion from such a small sampling. But I strongly suspect these responses are more typical than non-typical of Black unwed adolescent fathers. I know in my many years of experience with this population, young Black males would make similar remarks. In most cases of Black teenage pregnancy, the Black teenage male is branded as the uncaring culprit who is more concerned with his own sexual gratification than with the outcome of his act. To some extent, I agree he deserves this label because I know of few cases of teenage pregnancy where the teen male desired to have a child prior to intercourse. His female partner, on the other hand, often harbors such a desire. But the Black teen male's insatiable appetite for sex does not preclude him from having affections for a child born out of wedlock. Granted upon hearing the announcement that he is an expectant father will be a shock to him and cause him to have unexpected anxieties, fears, and frustrations, nonetheless, I sincerely believe that once the child is born, most Black teen males are affectionate and caring of the baby.

As we can deduce from the responses in the table, the respondents did show a concern for the care and welfare of their children. This is contrary to the popular belief that Black unwed adolescent fathers are unconcerned about their children. It is difficult, however, for most Black unwed adolescent fathers to help support their children. Due to their lack of skills and limited education, they have few marketable assets. And they face double jeopardy because of the constant high unemployment among Black youth.

Dr. Hendricks' study also revealed the following:

—there exist limited data on the needs and problems of Black unwed adolescent fathers;

—most respondents indicated they would seek help from their mothers, even when there was a father in the home;

—most felt they should be accountable for their act;

—85% showed an interest in school and got along well with their teachers;

—few respondents felt that their peers could provide them with support;

—most of the respondents would not take their problems to the clergy (Note: the majority were not church members);

—none of the respondents would seek assistance

—however, 95% responded in the affirmative when asked if they would attend an agency which offered parenting services to unwed fathers.[13]

Dr. Hendricks cites the last finding as the most important one in the study:

> The main implication to emerge from this study relates to the findings that ninety-five percent of the young fathers expressed a high degree of readiness to attend a teenage parenting agency if it offered services for unwed adolescent fathers. Therefore, agencies and institutions serving family planning needs should provide services for unwed adolescent mothers. If agencies and institutions provided such services to unmarried adolescent fathers, it would be a vital source of community social support for them. Thus, the unwed adolescent father may not, as a result of an unwanted pregnancy, feel overwhelmed, rejected, and frustrated in his move toward the attainment of his life goals.[14]

Dr. Hendricks' study indicates that greater community awareness and concern for Black unwed adolescent fathers would do much to improve their self-esteem and chances to become "responsible" fathers. One program that addresses itself to these issues is conducted by the ALPHA Fraternity, a national Black Greek Letter organization. This program provides orientation seminars for unwed teen fathers which emphasizes male responsibility and parenting skills. In addition it provides counseling services and adult role models for the participants. Such programs are greatly needed to help change the image of the irresponsible and uncaring male that has been labeled on so many Black fathers. If Black unwed adolescent fathers are to reverse this image, they must become more involved in the rearing and caring of their children despite the inequities they face. However, we should not expect these youths to assume responsible adult roles when most have not developed neither the maturity or social status to function as stable fathers. Until we can significantly reduce Black teenage pregnancies, the ultimate responsibility for rearing children born out of wedlock must be shared by the entire Black community.

Fortunately for Black teenage mothers, the Black community has, in recent years, become more responsive to their needs. In many Black communities today, there are programs which offer pre-natal and post-natal care, parenting education, family counseling, and other important life support systems to teenage mothers. One such program is the Sisterhood of Black Single Mothers, Inc. in Brooklyn. Founded in 1974 as a voluntary organization by Daphine Busby, the Sisterhood assists teenage mothers in returning to school and improving their parenting skills with the assistance of older single mothers. The program has the following goals:

—to pair a single "big sister" with a little sister who will serve as a positive role model and not as a disciplinarian;

—to improve the young mother's ability and willingness to interact with her child;

—to enhance her self-image, which will increase the likelihood of success in the school and work environment.[15]

To achieve these goals the Sisterhood provides a range of support systems which include peer counseling information and referrals; free clothing co-op; a youth awareness project; and the BIG APPLE project which is an acronym for Brooklynites Involved in Getting Adolescent Parents Positive Living Environments. The success of the Sisterhood has spurred other communities to replicate its program. The National Urban League is another organization which has placed teenage pregnancy high on its list of priorities. In addressing this problem, it has developed a school based model for teen pregnancy prevention and a community based model called Project Redirection that services pregnant teenagers and young mothers. Both programs are being implemented in a number of cities where Black teenage pregnancies are highly visible.

Despite programs such as the Sisterhood, the problem of Black teenage pregnancies persist. What is needed beside effective treatment programs are programs which can prevent this problem from becoming a fixed norm in the Black community. Even the best programs will fall short of reducing teenage pregnancies until the Black community is able to dramatically curb their frequency. Dr. Frances Cress Welsing puts it more bluntly:

> A people who cannot stop and prevent their children from giving birth to children and who do not understand the short and long term implications of their children giving birth to children and who do not understand the short and long term implications of their children giving birth to children are a people who are already far into their own HOLOCAUST and GENOCIDE.[16]

Dr. Welsing is not only critical of the teenage pregnancy problem, but also offers an alternative to resolve it in her Welsing Black Child Bearing Formula.

> Black teenage persons reproducing life must be totally prevented at the 100% level ... because of the conditions of racism (white supremacy), which means maximum level environmental stress on Black people in particular and all other non-white peoples, for the specific purpose of Black inferiorization and white genetic survival, Black people must engage in a conscious counter-offensive to ensure their maximum development of the Black genetic and constitutional potential by adopting the following, 'Welsing Black Child Bearing Formula:'

> That under the conditions of white supremacy, Black people should not think of marriage before the very late twenties; no children until the thirties and then no more than two, to which the mother and the father then commit the next twenty-five years of their lives to combating racism and structuring the conditions for maximal development of the genetic and constitutional potential of the two offsprings.

> Prior to marriage in the late twenties, the individual engages in self growth and development and a completed education.

Instead of the term "marriage," perhaps we Blacks should use the expression "commitment" to countering racism and to establish and maintain the future Black generations at the highest possible level of development.[17]

As dramatic as Dr. Welsing's formula may appear to some, when closely examined, one will find that it does contain a logical rationale in view of the long-term negative impact teenage pregnancies will have on the Black community. I personally feel that dramatic alternatives to the Black teenage pregnancy problem should not be ignored when we weigh the inevitable negative outcomes of this problem as it affects the future of Black people. As I have already indicated, these outcomes will produce a new generation of dysfunctional Black youth who will contribute little to the Black community and/or become wards of racist institutions, i.e., prisons, mental hospitals, drug and alcohol clinics, and the myriad of social agencies which comprise our dehumanizing welfare system. Because of the tremendous disadvantages placed on children of teen parents, the laws of probability make my prognosis a conservative one. Furthermore, I do not feel that Dr. Welsing's formula for regulating Black births negates the importance we should place on Black children. On the contrary, it would reconfirm our genuine concern for their welfare, and demonstrate that we are fully committed to the positive development of those who are born into this bittersweet world. Black Americans must chart their destinies along lines which are parallel to our goal of liberation. This means we must do those things which are in the best interest of the collective majority and which raises our chances to be totally free of oppression. At this period in our struggle, we must be selective, creative, and committed to doing not what may be "natural" but what is "sensible."

The needs of the Black community will not be answered simply by an increase in the Black population. What is needed is a generation of highly developed and political conscious youth who are dedicated to eradicating racism and oppression. The liberation of Black people will come as a result of the quality of our race and not in its numbers. This will never happen so long as we continue to have "babies raising babies."

On the contrary, when we ensure the positive development of all Black youth, our goal of liberation will have a greater chance of being achieved.

CHAPTER SEVEN

"THREE HOTS AND A COT"
THE HOAX OF THE MILITARY

> ... for most of its history the
> nation's military has been a white
> bastion whose personnel policies
> mirrored the racial prejudices
> prevalent in the rest of society.
>
> *Blacks and the Military*

The options available to today's Black youths are dwindling in numbers and often restricted to sources which are not always in their best interest. This is especially typical of those who are lacking in skills; disenfranchised from economic opportunities; alienated from critical life support systems; and who are compelled to survive on their impulses and street wise ingenuity. Unless these youths choose to live under these marginal circumstances, which usually lead to self-destructive behavior, they opt to find refuge in some institution they feel will buffer their hardship. One institution that has benefited from this desperation is America's self-proclaimed guardian of the free world—the United States Armed forces. Since the beginning of the ill-fated Viet Nam war, Black youths have been drawn to the armed forces in numbers which have dramatically surpassed past Black military quotas. To ensure that these numbers continue to swell the ranks of the military, the Armed Forces has entered the commercial market with a proliferation of exciting and over glamourized TV commercial and newspaper advertisement to promote its product as being "Number One." Using the slogans "Be the Best You Can Be," and "It's A Great Place To Start," each branch of the Pentagon's war machine is making a pitch to young Americans to take advantage of the opportunities each allege to offer. A sampling of some of these enticing commercials are as follows:

Ad #1

You've You've got it   You've got it together.
they'll see in a glance
Thanks to the Services
you got the chance
in the Army, Navy,
Air Force, Marines.

Looking for an opportunity to develop and grow as a person?
You'll find it in the Army, Navy, Air Force and Marines.
And that's especially true if you're smart enough to graduate from high school.
You can earn responsibility in the Services. Learn to lead.

Prove that you can make it. In fact, there are all kinds of opportunities for advancement.

The Armed Forces can bring out the best in you—actually help you grow better. For instance, there's even a program in which the government contributes money toward a college education.

Serving in the Armed Forces is an adventure and a challenge. There are new places to see and new friends to make.

Pay is higher than ever—more than $550 a month to start. And you can earn 30 days of vacation each year. Plus, the Services take care of your food, uniforms, housing and medical needs.

But above all, you'll gain new confidence, stand a little taller, walk a little prouder. All while serving your country. And that's one of the finest things a person can do.

To find out more, see your local Armed Forces recruiter or write Armed Forces Opportunities, P.O. Box C 1776, Huntington Station, N.Y. 11746

IT'S A GREAT PLACE TO START

Ad #2

AIM HIGH

Reach for new horizons

It's never easy. But reaching for new horizons is what aiming high is all about. Because to reach for new horizons you must have the vision to see things not only as they are, but as they could be. You must have the courage to accept new challenges.

The history of the Air Force is a history of men and women reaching for new horizons, dedicating their vision and courage to make our nation great.

You can join us in our quest for new horizons. Our pay and benefits are better than ever, with opportunities for growth and challenge.

Aim High: find out more. See your Air Force recruiter today or call toll free 1-800-423-USAF (in California 1-800-232-USAF). Better yet, mail in the card.

AIR FORCE A Great Way Of Life

Ad #3

95 BRAVO Military Police

Law enforcement is a tough and demanding field. But if you have what it takes to become a "95 Bravo," you'll be a member of our Military Police force and have the responsibility of protecting an entire Army. From police work to construction work, the Army has career training in over 300 areas, so you can serve your country in the way that best suits your talents. And if you qualify, we'll guarantee your choice of training. So if it's not 95 Bravo, maybe you should investigate 16 X-ray.*

ARMY

Be All You Can Be

*Air Defense. For more information, call toll free 1-800-USA-ARMY

If one would take these commercials seriously he may arrive at the romantic conclusion that the Armed Forces are, in fact, "a great place to start." And why not? They offer excitement, adventure, travel, free clothing, educational opportunities, a monthly pay check, and of course "three hots and a cot." Compared to what is available in civilian life to most Black youths, this is an offer too good to turn down. As a consequence, many Black youths are lured by the over glamourization of the armed forces and envision the military as being a replica of Disneyworld. Recruiters do little to correct this romantic illusion because they are more concerned in making quotas than making sense. Many parents, too, are duped by this hoax, and are often more than eager to approve of their teenagers embarking on a career of "military prosperity." And because of the difficulties and financial strain posed by teenagers, some parents are willing to approve their enlistment just to get rid of them.

My concern over the commercialization of the Armed

Forces to entice youths to enlist in one of its branches of service is not because the military is a despotic institution whose primary mission is to train men and women to protect this country's so-called democratic way of life from unfriendly nations. This is a mission all nations must have as their highest priority in view of the conflicts which have historically marked relationships among nations who hold opposing ideologies, not to mention the imperialistic lust of those nations who seek power just for the sake of power. The number of wars fought among nations have been astronomical and only those that have successfully maintained their military superiority are able to "reap the spoils" and survive on their own terms. On the contrary, my concern over the rash of Black youths who are now entering the Armed Forces is the motive for their enlistment which, in most cases, I feel is predicated on the limited options available to them in civilian life. When Black youths have little hope in gaining meaningful employment, and find themselves faced with the dilemma of "to survive or not to survive" without engaging in criminal acts, the choice of enlisting in the military becomes an attractive one. At least in the military you can be assured of having "three hots and a cot" and a monthly pay check.

> Military pay and benefits, job training and educational assistance, and social opportunities are particularly attractive to black youth; for many, in fact, the armed forces have provided their only opportunity for escape from ghetto (colony) life and from possible participation in the nation's underground economy.[1]

Harry Edwards identifies another factor that makes the military attractive to Black male youths. He calls it the "manhood hustle" which feeds on the egoes of young Black males.

> A manhood hustle perpetrated by military recruitment officers contributes to Blacks joining the more dangerous elite military units (such as the paratroopers and special forces) far in excess of what proportionately would be expected...[2]

There are other issues which I feel should also be considered when appraising the high enlistment rate of Black youths in the military.

1. The racial composition of today's military shows that Blacks comprise a greater proportion of its population than any other ethnic group.

2. In the last two wars in both Korea and Viet Nam, Black soldiers had a higher percentage of casualties than any other ethnic group.

3. After enlisting in the military many Black youths learn that although they receive "three hots and a cot," they are still victimized by institutional racism.

4. There is a high percentage of Black youths who leave the military with other than honorable discharges.

5. A large number of Black youths who return to civilian life only to find that their chances for success are not better than they were when they enlisted in the military.

6. Does the military provide Black youths with the type of socialization they need to successfully complete their "rites of passage?"

These issues should be of great concern to the Black community. They represent another reason why Black youths are becoming an endangered species and are being displaced in institutions which are insensitive to their exceptional needs. In recent years, the military has become one of the most prominent institutions which affect the socialization of Black youths. Although it does provide for their basic needs, the military serves as a guise that veils one of America's most notable contradictions; a Black can die for his country but still be denied his fundamental rights. This contradiction has typified the military and has yet to be fully resolved. To appraise the impact of the military on Blacks, however, it is necessary to briefly review it from a historical perspective. From its inception, the American military was racist in practice if not in its original purpose.

In the original militias of colonial America every available man—white or black, freed-man or slave—was to help defend the domestic order against Indian uprisings, European transgressors, and other threats to peace. However, colonial leaders soon realized that domestic order was constantly threatened by the possibility of slave revolts. Persuaded by the fear that free Black militiamen might support such institutions and a related apprehension about training slaves in the use of arms, the American colonies developed a policy of excluding Blacks from military services.[3]

To ensure that Blacks would adhere to this policy, the colonies enacted exclusionary laws in 1637 to prohibit them from military obligation "least our slaves when armed might become our masters." Later, some of these laws were modified to accommodate some Blacks to serve as drummers, laborers, and in other non-combatant positions. Despite these restrictions, Blacks still managed to make their presence felt in America's early wars with the Indians (although some fought alongside the Indians) and later in the American Revolution. It is estimated that nearly 5,000 Black militiamen fought alongside the colonists during this epic conflict. It should also be noted that many Blacks joined or supported the British army as the better of two evils.

The armed colonials the Southern blacks saw were slave catchers' patrols. It was not irrational to choose the devil you did not know. This would explain why many free as well as slave blacks sided with the British.[4]

The primary motive for Blacks fighting with either the colonists or the British was their hope that being on the victor's side would gain them respect and freedom. The following statement epitomizes the feelings of many Blacks who believed that fighting for America was the just and sensible thing to do.

Shall he go to war and fight for the country's flag? Yes, yes, for every reason of true patriotism, it is a blessing in disguise for the Negro. He will if for no other reason be possessed of arms, which in the South in the face of threatened mob violence he is not allowed to have. He will become trained and disciplined. He will be generously renumerated for his services. He will get much honor. He will have an opportunity of proving to the world his real bravery, worth and manhood.[5]

Contrary to this belief, they did not get the respect they longed for. When the colonists became victorous, this hope was quickly jaded as the heroics of Black soldiers went unappreciated and they were returned to the plantation.

Although Blacks were excluded from combat during the early stages of the Civil War, before the war ended nearly 390,000 fought in this conflict, the greatest number in the North. Of this number, there were over 38,000 casualties, a mortality rate that was 40 percent higher than that of white troops. A sizable number of the Black casualties that occurred was not the result of combat but due to the poor treatment, bad medical care, and inadequate equipment they were subjected to. Despite their bravery during the Civil War, when it was over, Black soldiers again returned to their homes still denied the freedoms which they had fought for. At the end of the Civil War, Blacks comprised ten percent of the military, and there were six Black regiments authorized by Congress. These regiments saw considerable duty during the Indian Wars, and many distinguished themselves as the much feared and renowned Buffalo Solders.

For ten years they fought the Comanches, Kiowas, Arapahos, Sioux and the Southern Cheyenne and spent another 10 years taming the fierce Apaches of New Mexico and Arizona. They patroled the Mexican border and rid it of bandits and revolutionaries, rode up San Juan Hill in the Spanish American War and ousted the boomers, illegal settlers from the plains.[6]

Around the turn of the 20th century, the military began to grudgingly acknowledge the achievements of Black troops, although it remained segregated as ever. One problem that persistently confronted the military was the stationing of Black troops, particularly in the state of Texas. This problem was highlighted by two infamous incidents which resulted in a number of Black troops being killed or court martialed. In 1906, Black soldiers stationed in Brownsville, Texas were accused of shooting a white person and starting a riot. Although the charges were never proven, President Theodore Roosevelt ordered the dishonorable discharge of 167 Black soldiers. Later evidence revealed that the Black soldiers were innocent, but it was not until 1972 did the Department of the Army amend for its misdeed and changed the discharges to honorable. The incident in 1917 in Houston, Texas was even more outrageous. The whites there adamantly resented Black soldiers being stationed in Houston and their feelings eventually ignited a race riot after an altercation between Black soldiers and white policemen. As in the Brownsville incident, the Black soldiers were held responsible and 118 indicted and convicted of murder. Nineteen were secretly hanged and sixty three sentenced to life imprisonment. The remaining soldiers received dishonorable discharges.

Despite these and other incidents of flagrant mistreatment in the military, many Blacks continued to enlist in the service because they believed that military life offered them greater opportunities than in civilian life. In addition, many Blacks still held a sense of patriotism that ignored America's failure to provide them equal justice. But some of this faith was diluted when Black soldiers returned home after World War I to find that American racism remained the same. The trend of racial injustice continued in the armed forces for decades to follow. Black soldiers were systematically relegated to menial positions, and were almost virtually excluded from the so-called elite services such as the navy, marines, and air force. In fact, there were no Blacks in the Marine Corps before 1918, and the Navy had less than one percent. Even during World War II, quotas were placed on Blacks, and they continued to be treated like military misfits.

Black women did not become active in the military until World War II. But like Black males they, too, were segregated in all areas of military life.

> During the 1940s and 1950s, Black service women were subjected to open and hidden forms of discrimination and segregation. In the Army and Air Force a few white male base commanders were openly unwilling to assign Black women to semi-skilled or technical jobs.[7]

It was not until 1948, when President Harry S. Truman issued an executive order which "declared to be the policy of the President ·that there shall be equality of treatment and opportunity for all persons in the armed services without regard to race, color, or natural origin," that Blacks were given any type of assurance they would be treated as equal to their white counterparts. But the racist tradition of America remained true to form, and Blacks in the military were still treated, for the most part, like misfits. Simply, the armed forces were/are in fact an extension of the institutional racism that has become synonymous with the "American way of life." The military maintained its institutional racism through the early years of the Korean War until it became apparent to the Department of Defense that a desegregated armed forces was in its best interest. With this belated decision, the military began to integrate its services on a token basis which persisted until the end of the war. After the Korean War there was an upsurge in Black enlistees and by 1951 one out of every four recruits in the Army was Black. Eventually in a report entitled "Project Clear," the Army concluded that total desegregation was the only way American could maintain an effective military.

The Army should commit itself to a policy of integration to be carried out as rapidly as operational efficiency permits.[8]

Before this report, the Air Force and Navy had already integrated their services, and, for the first time in its history, America had a bona fide integrated armed forces. The increase of Blacks in the military began to peak at the beginning of the Viet Nam War, and the Department of Defense's statistics revealed that Blacks were more likely to (1) be drafted, (2) be sent to Viet Nam, (3) serve in high risk combat units and consequently (4) be killed or wounded in battle. This prophesy was borne out by the fact that between 1961 and 1966, Black casualties accounted for one-fourth of all losses in Viet Nam. Furthermore, the Department of Defense claimed this was unavoidable because most Black soldiers could not qualify for the highly skilled jobs, and therefore, were invariably assigned to combat units where they only needed to learn the skill of killing. Some Black organizations challenged this rationale, and claimed that military tests were racially bias and the Department of Defense was conspiring against young Black males. Nonetheless, Blacks continued to be disproportionately represented in high risk combat areas, and were a formidable force in America's most tainted and unpopular war. The effects of Viet Nam were devastating to all those who fought in this unjustifiable war, but for many young Blacks they were a revelation in betrayal and horror.

Wallace Terry, a Black journalist who covered the Viet Nam War for Time Magazine, has recorded a thoroughly provocative and insightful oral narrative of the experiences of 20 Black soldiers who served in Viet Nam. Their experiences are told with no punches spared and constitute a major document that should be read by every Black youth. Following are excerpts from seven of these narratives that reveal not only the horror of war but its psychological and racist impact on the psyches of their narrators.

"You didn't have white friends. White people were the aliens to me. This is "63." You don't have integration really in the South. You expected them to treat you bad. But somehow in the Marine Corps you hoping all that's gonna change. Of course, I found out this was not true, because the Marine Corps was the last service to integrate. And I had an Indian for a platoon commander who hated Indians. He used to call Indians blanket ass. And when we had a Southerner from Arkansas they liked to call you chocolate bunny and Brillo head. That kind of shit."[9]

"But I got to find out that white people weren't as tough, weren't the number one race and all them other perceptions that they had tried to ingrain in my head. I found out they got scared like I did. I found out a lot of them were a lot more cowardly than I expected. I found out some of them were more animalistic than any black people I knew. I found out that they really didn't have their shit together."[10]

"You know, they decorated me in Viet Nam. Two Bronze Stars. The whiteys did. I was wounded three times. The officers, the generals, and whoever came out to the hospital

to see you. They respected you and pat you on the back.
They said, 'You brave. And you courageous. You America's
finest. America's best.' Back in the States the same officers
that pat me on the back wouldn't even speak to me. They
wanted that salute, that attention, 'til they holler at ease. I
didn't get the respect that I thought I was gonna get."[11]

"My sister's husband was with me. He got shrapnel in his
eye. His vision is messed up. There were 2,000 people in the
church. And the pastor gave us space to talk, 'cause we
were the only two that went to Vietnam. My brother-in-law
is a correction officer at the jail. So we've always been kind
of aggressive. Ain't scared that much. But we got up there
to talk, and we couldn't do nothing but cry. My wife cried.
My children cried. The whole church just cried."[12]

"When I was in Vietnam, it was not important to me where
I died. Now it is very important to me. I made a promise in
'Nam that I would never risk my life or limb to protect
anybody else's property. I will protect my own. So this
country is not going to tell me to go out again to stop the
spread of communism. In Germany we were buying beef
for the GI's that came from Communist countries."[13]

"My personal feeling is that black people have problems
and still have problems in America. But I never told them
that, because I had not intention of helping them to defeat
us. We deal with our problems within our own country.
Some people just do not live up to the great ideals our
country stands for. And some blacks don't take advantage
of the privileges and opportunities we have. Although
black people are kind of behind the power curtain, we have
just as much claim to this country as any white man.
America is the black man's best hope."[14]

"These men belonged to a generation that was far, far more
outspoken than any generation of black men before them.
So they get over there, get introduced to the drugs, the
killings, the uncertainty, and they still had to put up with
racism within the service. They were there to kill and be
killed. About ready to die. To do first-class dying. Yet in
terms of their assignments and promotions and awards,

they were getting second-class treatment. It created a special brand of bitterness.

And many of them came back home with less than honorable discharges, caused by their anger and outspokeness. So they lost their veterans' benefits, which weren't so great anyway. I don't think you can call Vietnam a success story for the young blacks who served there. A few stayed in service and did very well. But those who experienced the racism in the war we lost wear a scar. Vietnam left a scar on them that won't go away. The black soldier paid a special price."[15]

From reading these brief excerpts, it becomes obvious that even an integrated armed forces pose many problems to Blacks. And perhaps the most serious of these problems is the paradox faced by Black service men and women who are willing to fight and die for a freedom that is denied them.

As unpopular as the Viet Nam War was, one would think that this in itself would be a deterrent to enlistment. On the contrary, after Congress passed a bill in 1973 to have an All-Volunteer Armed Forces, new enlistees soared to unprecedented numbers; a large percentage of them being Black. The Army was the largest benefactor of this escalation in enlistment, and in 1981, 1 out of every 3 soldiers was Black. Considering that Blacks make up approximately 10% of the national census, this ratio was significantly higher than what Congress anticipated or wanted.

Congress, however, continues to be concerned that the Armed Forces may be becoming disproportionately composed of individuals who have lower socio-economic status or who are members of racial/ethnic (Black) minorities.[16]

As I have already indicated, for many Black youths the military offered the only alternative to an otherwise life of unemployment, disenfranchisement, and alienation. Little did these enlistees realize that many of these same things would continue to taunt them in the military. For many Black youths military life is a painful experience, and their difficulty to adjust to its rigid protocol and discipline often results in Blacks committing a higher percentage of crimes in the military than whites. The following chart delineates the crime rates of Black and white army personnel from 1978 to 1980.

CRIME RATES OF ARMY PERSONNEL BY RACE
FISCAL YEARS 1978-80

Rates per thousand

Category	1978 White	1978 Black	1979 White	1979 Black	1980 White	1980 Black
Crimes of violence[1]	2.8	12.7	2.8	11.8	3.1	11.8
Crimes against property[2]	10.1	17.6	9.9	18.9	12.8	22.1
Drug Offenses[3]	36.6	54.6	34.7	56.7	35.9	54.2

1. Includes murder, rape, aggravated assault, and robbery.
2. Includes burglary, larceny, auto theft, and housebreaking.
3. Includes use, possession, sale, and trafficking.[17]

Of all the disciplinary incidents, Blacks only have a lower precentage than whites on the act of desertion.

> The data show consistent differences: (1) males are far more apt than females to be AWOL or desert; (2) relatively more black males go AWOL but relatively fewer desert than their white counterparts; and (3) black females have the lowest incidence in both categories of indiscipline.[18]

From this statement we also learn that Black females are less likely to get into trouble than any other ethnic group regardless of gender. This suggests that Black females are better able to adjust to military life which may be due to a greater number choosing to make a career out of the military. Conversely, many Black male youths enlist in the military as a "bail out" from the depressed economic conditions in civilian life. However, as we have already shown, this "bail out" falls far short of compensating for these conditions when they return to civilian life.

Although the Department of Defense has, in recent years, tried to neutralize this over representation of Blacks in the Armed Forces, Blacks continue to be disproportionately represented in the military, particularly in the Army. Some people feel that there is nothing wrong with this skewed representation because the military does fill an economic void for many Black youth. No doubt some Black youths do benefit from their experiences in the military after discharge, although there are no formal studies which have tracked their post-military occupational careers to confirm this. But it is my guess those Black youths from this group would have fared well in civilian life even if they had not entered the military. Of course for those Black youths who aspire to attend college, qualify for any of the highly skilled jobs or enter officer training, these benefits are especially enticing. Yet the vast majority of Black youths enlist in the service, today, as a means of economic survival.

> Though black youth may find different features of the military the most appealing, the common factor that influences its overall attractiveness, particularly to young black males, is the dismal civilian labor market that confronts them.[19]

There is a more fundamental question Black youths should ask themselves before deciding to enlist in the military. This question becomes even more critical in view of the world tensions which find many Black and Third World Nations attempting to control their destinies in a climate of imperialistic intervention and expansion by powers of both the Western and Eastern bloc countries. El Salvador, Nicaragua, Uganda, Lebanon, Haiti, Ethiopia are just a few potential war zones which could find American soldiers implementing America's nebulous foreign policy. We have already seen America agitate a war in its reckless invasion of Grenada in October 1983. On the pretense of protecting U.S. citizens from an alleged assault by the Grenada government, President Reagan ordered 7,000 crack Marine and Ranger troops to descend on this small nation located near the southern tip of the Windwood Island chain to evacuate the Americans. A few months earlier Prime Minister Maurice Bishop and his top aides of the newly formed New Jewel Movement (NJM) were assassinated in a plot to overthrow the NJM's socialist government which some believed as CIA conspired. Plans for this invasion were orchestrated under the highest security, and when they were executed it was the first time in U.S. history that U.S. journalists were barred from the location where U.S. troops were fighting. In fact, the invasion of Grenada was so clandestinely executed that it has been impossible to confirm the number of either American or Grenadian casualties. One eyewitness report by a Black American living in Granada gave this account of the first day after the invasion.

> We are all numb from the savagery of it. Meanwhile tanks patrol the road outside. No way to bury the dead, attend to the wounded or even determine the casualties. We are all crazed prisoners in our own houses. My neighbors are keeping me sane. Perhaps we are keeping each other sane. But all around me is news of the dead, details of the dying. The children are silent, pitiful shadows of themselves. We are helpless to help them.[20]

On another day, the observer was awakened at dawn and reported the following scene:

> Instead, the people on the front lawn were U.S. Marines, about 40, many of them Black, baffled at finding U.S. citizens still on the island and caught in the line of fire.[21]

This observation should be extremely disturbing to every Black American, that is, Black soldiers fighting other people of African descent. War is tragic enough than to have brother killing brother because they happen to be citizens under different flags. No doubt some Black soldiers who participated in the invasion of Grenada thought exactly this. I seriously doubt if members of other ethnic groups will be placed in similar situations. Jews will never fight Jews; Irish will not fight Irish, nor will Poles fight Poles or Puerto Ricans fight Puerto Ricans. Granted these groups may have their intra-group conflicts, but it's inconceivable that those who are American citizens would ever participate in an invasion of their homeland. Although Grenada is not the (mother country) of Black Americans, it is a part of the Black Diaspora which is an extension of African's displaced millions. America has already come close to intervening in conflicts in Uganda, Zimbabwe, and Angola because of its vested interest. We must not forget its involvement in helping to fragmentize the revolutionary forces in the Congo before the assassination of Patrice Lumumba. And America must make its position unequivocably clear when the revolutionary Black forces in South Africa one day put the bastille of racism (apartheid) to its stanchest challenge. Although the chances of Black soldiers engaging in combat against their brothers and sisters may appear to be slim, the unpredictability of America's foreign policy makes even the slimest odds subject to an abrupt and radical change.

Black youths have every right to enlist in the military if this is what they really want to do. While I may have reservations about their decision to do so, this does not mean I totally disapprove of Black youths enlisting in the service. At times it may be a reasonable choice if Black youths fully understand the social and political implications of their decision. Unfortunately this is not usually the case, and as I already indicated, most Black youths enlist in the military because they have no other alternative. Once again we have a situation where the socialization of Black youths is influenced by white institutions which do not reflect the liberating needs of the Black community. No wonder many Black youths fail to acquire a sense of mission that is consistent and supportive of our struggle to determine our own destiny. The positive development of Black youth must be shaped and nurtured by Black institutions! Perhaps when we begin to provide our youths with such institutions, along with our uncompromising commitment to their social welfare, Black youths will have other more positive alternatives to select from than seeking sanctuary in the military.

CHAPTER EIGHT

"HI MOM!":
THE JOCK STRAP MENTALITY

> Every black amateur athlete
> dreams of "turning pro." In his
> mind it is almost as if the natural
> progression of things is to play
> high school sports, receive an
> athletic grant-in-aid to some big
> name college, and after four years
> of collegiate stardom, to sign a
> whopping bonus contract with
> some professional team.
>
> Dr. Harry Edwards
> *The Revolt of The Black Athlete*

The stadium was packed to capacity despite the adverse weather conditions that had spectators wrapped in a variety of winter clothing to protect them from the brutal cold. Pandemonium began to set in and all of the excitement of America's favorite winter sport came into focus on this brawny December afternoon. But this was not unusual for a football game between two national collegiate powers, for the craze for the sport has become a spectator's delight and an athlete's obsession. For those who could not attend this thrilling event, there was the technology of television to filter the excitement into the homes of untold millions.

The game was in the last minute with the team in possession three points behind. The clock continued to move as the players left their huddle and assumed a strong side spread formation. At the snap of the ball, the wide receiver accelerated off the line and avoided the hand check of a defensive back and sped down the sidelines. When he approached the 10 yard line he was confronted by the free safety whom he successfully out maneuvered. The quarterback seeing his receiver in the clear hurled a long spiral pass that found its target on the tip of the receiver's fingers who then proceeded to cross the goal line unmolested. Immediately after touching the end zone, the receiver spiked the ball against the frigid turf. In less than two seconds he was surrounded by teammates who almost knocked him off his feet in their zealous celebration. Untangling himself from his spirited teammates, the receiver caressed the ball in his arms and dashed to the side lines where he was again greeted by teammates and even a few coaches. Finally, after the extra point was kicked successfully, he made his way to the bench and wrapped a blanket around his well-built frame. Then as though he knew that the cameras were focusing on him, he turned to give the TV audience a broad smile, raised his right index finger to signal that his team is number one and in a deep baritone shouted "Hi, Mom!" His smile continued to be visible as the TV cameras attempted to capture all of his ecstasy to allow the millions of spectators across the country to see this game breaker offer acknowledgement to his mother.

The scene which I have described is one that every athlete, regardless of the sport he plays, looks forward to making a sensational play that provides him an opportunity to salute his mother on national TV. Seldom do these occasions see an athlete acknowledging the father. Instead, "Hi, Mom", becomes the standard gesture for the great majority of athletes. While some people may try to diagnose this ritual as an extension of the Oedipus Complex Syndrome (if there is such a thing), it is described here mainly as an introduction to the "Jock Strap Mentality."

The term is not a novel one. It has been used in crowded locker rooms and among athletes and coaches for many years. In its most generic interpretation, the term "Jock Strap Mentality" implies that a person is so obsessed with athletics that his mind is obstructed to any other influence. Furthermore, the obsession becomes so binding that it begins to regulate the person's life style and value system. As a result, the person is so mesmerized by its appeal, his entire world becomes a conglomerate of footballs, baseballs, basketballs, etc. And in his enthusiasm to excel in his chosen sport, the person is almost willing to sacrifice his total being to become efficient in it. Dramatic as this may sound, there is sufficient evidence to suggest that a disproportionate number of Black youths are addicted to the "Jock Strap Mentality." This addiction has been so pervasive that for many Black youths a career in athletics is often seen as the only alternative to help them overcome their lowly life status. Poverty, discrimination, lack of education, lack of training, and lack of cultural supports mean this: most careers, while theoretically open to blacks, are closed to them in reality. The black community knows this, and so blacks flow into sports as the Irish, Italians and Jews went into boxing during earlier times and just as Hispanics now flow into baseball and boxing.

Although Black youths in America have historically been attracted to sports, this attraction has greatly accelerated in the past 30 years. When Jackie Robinson broke into the lily-white major league in 1945, a new era began for Black athletes. Prior to this time, Black athletes had been relegated to their own less publicized athletic organizations and were not accepted as "mainstream athletes." Thus a Satchel Paige was not rated in the same class of Bob Fellow; nor Marquis Haynes with a

Bob Cousy; or Black collegiate coaches like Big House Gaines of Winston Salem Teachers College and Jake Gaither of Florida A&M with an Adolph Rupp of Kentucky or a Bear Bryant of Alabama.

"America went through a depression and two wars with its black-white collegiate separation unbroken, with the notable exceptions of Paul Robeson, Kenny Washington and Jackie Robinson. But with the end of World War II and the new orientations that this catastrophic event wrought, hitherto all-white schools began to reassess their policies of excluding black students in general and black athletes in particular."[1]

As Black athletes enrolled in the sports programs of white colleges, they quickly became dominant figures, and for the first time Black youth could view on national TV Black athletes running for touchdowns, scoring points in basketball and hitting home runs. No doubt this exposure greatly increased the insatiable interest Black youth already had in sports. This desire has been responsible for Blacks becoming prominent in most major sports, except tennis, golf and hockey.

...nearly 100 percent of heavyweight boxers are black, as are approximately 60 percent of professional basketball players, 40 percent of professional football players, and 20 percent of professional baseball players.[2]

These figures would increase even more if not for the racial quotas most professional and collegiate teams impose to regulate their number of Black athletes. However, no quota could restrain the exceptional skills of the Black athlete and Black "superstars" have flourished in most professional and collegiate sports.

...Black basketball players score 12 percent more points and get 10 more rebounds than white players. Black running backs gain 17 percent more yards and score 100 percent more touchdowns than white running backs. The lifetime batting average of black baseball players is 7 percent higher than that of white players.[3]

Today, it is estimated that approximately 75% of Black

youths engage in some type of formal or informal sport. This participation can be seen throughout America in both rural and urban communities. The most prominent sports among Black youths are baseball, softball, basketball, football, boxing, and track and field, although not necessarily in this order. Other popular sports such as hockey, volleyball, golf and tennis have lesser appeal probably due to the inaccessibility of proper physical resources and economic restrictions. The latter two big money sports have produced few outstanding Black athletes. The cost for grooming competitive tennis and golf players is extremely high and therefore, these sports are for all intents and purposes exclusively white. Only a hand full of Black athletes have stood out in these racist sports: Althea Gibson and Arthur Ashe in tennis and Lee Elder in golf.

In 1983, the Miller Lite Brewing Company published its study on the influence of sports on American life. The study was conducted by the independent research firm of Research and Forecasts, Inc., and is based on extensive data gathered in a nationwide survey of 1,319 men, women and teenagers, and augmented by interviews with 410 coaches, sports writers, broadcasters and sports physicians. The study is considered to be the most comprehensive and exhaustive research ever done on the status of sports in America. An extrapolation of some of its major findings as they relate to Black youths reveal the following:

1. A majority of Americans (6690) believe there are more opportunities in sports than in other fields for the social advancement of Blacks and other minorities.

2. 51% of the survey expressed their belief that organized sports helps integration and reduces racial tensions.

3. A substantial majority (7490) believe that athletes make good role models for children; 5990 said they are the best models.

4. Most adults (82%) believe that sports participation by youth greatly reduced crime. However, only a third (34%) of the teenagers shared this view.

5. 75% felt that children should be encouraged to engage in sports.

6. 92% believed competition is good for children because it teaches them to strive to do their best.

7. One of every three persons (34%) interviewed dreamt of becoming a professional athlete rather than a famous movie star, internationally known scientist or statesman.

The above findings are interesting for many reasons, however, three stand out to be the most significant in helping to explain the "Jock Strap Mentality."

1. The belief that sports provide greater opportunities for Blacks.

2. The belief that sports can be a cure for racism and reduce crime.

3. The belief that athletes are the best role models for children.

These beliefs are probably shared to a large degree by many members of the Black community. And with the massive commercial glamorization of professional athletes, it is little wonder black youths become so attracted to sports.

The media serves as the vehicle which carries the fantasies consumed by youth Black males. Few media items are consumed more completely by the Black male than professional sports. Professional sports are perceived as being the short cut to the pinnacle of American society. The professional athlete enjoys "the long bread" a "bad new ride" plus a high degree of social acceptance. A young Black male struggling to develop a positive self concept in a racist society can turn on the TV set and see Black athletes being cheered and sought after by fans and reporters.[4]

(Quote taken from an unpublished paper by Dr. John C. Gaston titled *The Destruction of the Young Black Male: The Impact of Popular Culture and Organized Sports*)

However, the road to athletic prominence is more difficult than most Black youths ever imagine. And for the few who do make it, the careers of Black athletes are far less glamorous than what they are led to believe. A review of two major sports, basketball and football, will illustrate these points. Of an estimated 700,000 high school basketball players in a given year, only 15,000 are eligible for NCAA athletic scholarships. Of the approximate 4,000 basketball players who complete their collegiate basketball careers in a given year, only 200 will be drafted by the NBA teams, which have room for only 50 rookies. In football, it is estimated that over one million high school youth play the game each year; yet there are only 41,000 scholarships available to them. At the professional level, 320 are drafted each year in the NFL with openings for only 150. Although this number will change because of the newly organized USFL, I do not feel the difference will be that significant in view of the exceptional large numbers who seek professional careers. About ten million Black male youths dream of getting one of the only three thousand jobs for players. You don't have to be a statistician to know that those odds are ludicrous.

When these figures are closely examined, it becomes clear that professional sports do not comprise the most viable occupational opportunities for Black youth. On the contrary, the odds for achievement in professional sports are far greater than those for becoming a doctor, chemist or an engineer. In addition, the physical abuse occurred by many professional athletes often have a lasting and debilitating effect on their lives. The average career for professional football players is 4.2 seasons, for basketball players, it is 3.4 seasons. So even if the average Black professional earns $50,000 (a high average) each year during these periods, he is not likely to have saved any money when his career comes to an abrupt end. Since the majority of Black professional athletes fail to complete their college education, they reenter the world of reality as though they were having a nightmare. Few are able to gain meaningful employment and even Black superstars seldom get the types of lucrative jobs and endorsement contracts provided to less talented white athletes.

Despite these grim facts, (which are not always known to Black youths) Black youths continue to pound the basketball for countless hours and practice the moves of Walter Payton over and over again in their aspirations to become professional athletes. The dedication and commitment Black youth give to these sports are truly remarkable. One can only speculate what Black youths could accomplish if this boundless energy were redirected to other meaningful endeavors.

In fact, few occupations or professions demand so much of one's time to achieve success as does the preparation for a professional athletic career. And from a long-term perspective most occupations and professions are exceedingly more stable and durable. But those Black youth addicted with a "Jock Strap Mentality" cannot see beyond a basketball court or football field. Their total lives are centered around succeeding in athletics, and even when it is evident they will not achieve their goal, some continue to act out their ambition like a punch drunk boxer. Of all the sports admired by Black youth, basketball is the one most accessible to them. Because of its contained environment, basketball can be performed almost anywhere, consequently, sand lot basketball has become a fixture in the Black community.

For many Black youths, the lore of sand lot basketball is an indispensable part of their lifestyle in the ghetcolony. It is the center stage for showcasing one's physical attributes, cunniness and ability to survive. Indeed, it takes on the manifestations of a cult with its own rituals and set of rules.

> "Outdoor pick-up games rarely have referees. An honor system" is employed. If a man thinks he has fouled, he calls it himself and takes the ball out of bounds. This results in a lot of arguing. No one argued better than Eddie Simmons. "Guys would take the ball off him clean whistle," Hawk laughs, and "and Ed would holler, 'Foul!' He got away with it, cause he seemed so sure of himself."[5]

The "Hawk" mentioned in the above quote is the great Connie Hawkins, a product of Harlem who became a scapegoat for his alleged involvement in a basketball scandal that kept him out of the National Basketball Association for eight years. Connie Hawkins is typical of many oppressed Black youths who pursue basketball to compensate for other deficiencies, and to booster their damaged egos.

For many young men in the slums, the schoolyard is the only place they can feel true pride in what they do, where they can move free of inhibitions (even from coaches), where people applaud their accomplishments, and where they can by being spectacular rise, for the moment, above the drabness and anonymity of their lives, Thus, when a player develops extraordinary "schoolyard" moves and shots, these become more than simple athletic skills. They are an inseparable part of his personality. The level of his "game" becomes his measure as a man. So it was-and still is-with Connie.[6]

When Connie Hawkins was eventually exonerated after playing in the American Basketball League and with the Harlem Globetrotters, he became an NBA player. However, though he was still an exceptional athlete, Connie had lost some of his dazzling skills and was denied the super stardom that he rightfully deserved.

Sandlot basketball also played an important role in the development of Kareem Abdul-Jabbar, the perennial all-star center for the Los Angeles Lakers.

Just as white college basketball was patterned and regimented like the lives awaiting its players, the school-yard game demanded all the falsh, guile, and individual reckless brilliance each man would need in the world facing him. This was on-the-job training when no jobs were available. No wonder these games were so intense, so consuming and passionate. For a lot of the men on that court this was as good as it was ever going to get, and it was winner-stay-on. Who says the work ethic didn't live in the ghetto, that Calvinism and social Darwinism were outmoded credos? These were philosophers out there, every one-on-one a debate, each new move a breakthrough concept, every weekend another treatise. I took the seminar every chance I could.[7]

The list of Black superstars who served their apprenticeship in sandlot basketball is endless. In fact, most Black professional basketball players have been indoctrinated to the rigors of sandlot basketball. However, the vast majority of Black basketball players, including many outstanding ones, never graduate from its asphalt arena. Instead, they remain in the ghetcolony acting out their skills in their never ending desire to become professional athletes. But despite their dedication and talents, they face barriers which make it mathematically impossible for them to ever don a uniform of a professional athletic team. Still many persist in pursuing their dream, and it has been said that a recruiter could field a team of superstars from the playgrounds and schoolyards where raw talent can be seen daily executing behind the back passes, twisting jumpers and spectacular dunk shots. The following poetic lines provide a graphic summary of sandlot basketball's unique characteristics:

Basketball is the city game.

Its battlegrounds are strips of asphalt between tattered wire fences or crumbling buildings; its rhythms grow from the uneven thump or a ball against hard surfaces.

It demands no open spaces or lush backyards or elaborate equipment.

It doesn't even require specified numbers of players; a one-on-one confrontation in a playground can be as memorable as a full-scale organized game.

Basketball is the game for young athletes without cars or allowances-the game whose drama and action are intensified by its confined spaces and chaotic surroundings.[8]

As noted earlier, the odds against Black high school athletes becoming professionals are extraordinarily high. And while most talented high school athletes will get an opportunity to attend college, the percentage that graduate is pathetic. This is particularly true of those who attend predominantly white colleges. Despite their shortcomings, Black colleges are more successful in graduating their athletes. Most white colleges seem to be primarily concerned with the contributions Black athletes can make to their sports programs. As proprietors of gigantic athletic arenas, their priority is to sell tickets and receive lucrative TV contracts. It is simply a matter of economics, and to ensure that they fill quality teams, many colleges are willing to violate NCAA's recruiting and academic standards.

Some cases of athletic pampering by white colleges are outrageous. They range from the manipulation of manuscripts, under the table financial assistance to helping athletes meet minimum academic standards through unscrupulous means. Examples of these violations have been numerous and span over many years. One is being cited here to illustrate how they have damaged the careers of many gifted Black athletes.

Andre Logan was a 6 foot 7 inch forward from Andrew Jackson High School in Queens, New York who attended Mercer County Community College in Trenton before transferring to the University of New Mexico in 1978. At New Mexico he became a member of the varsity and had a promising future. However, in his senior year, it was discovered by the NCAA that his transcript had been falsified, and therefore he was declared ineligible. Later, evidence disclosed that he was unaware of this misdeed, when it was revealed that the athletic director and head coach conspired to make it appear he had made up a three credit deficiency. Four other members of the same team were suspended for similar reasons. When the evidence surfaced, the athletic director and coach were indicted and had to resign. But the careers of Andre Logan and his other team mates were never resumed because of the incident.

Regardless of the risks involved in violating NCAA standards, many college persist in breaking them. As a result a large percentage of Black athletes attend colleges merely to perform their athletic skills, and their status as students is of secondary concern. However, the price they pay for this "professional treatment" is extremely high.

First of all, there is no such thing as a "free ride." A black athlete pays dearly with his blood, sweat, tears and ultimately with some portion of his manhood, for the questionable right to represent his school on the athletic field. Second, the white athletic establishments on the various college campuses frequently fail to live up to even the most rudimentary responsibilities implied in their half of the agreement. As we have seen, the educational experiences of most black athletes on white college campuses would insult the intellectual aspirations of an idiot.[9]

Not all high school athletes are oblivious to these unsavory practices and some are willing to take their chances if they feel it might enhance their athletic aspirations. In Illinois, for example, a survey done in 1984 by the Chicago Sun Times of the top 43 senior prospects in the state revealed the following:

Eighty-eight percent believe most colleges cheat, that they will do "almost anything" to recruit a bluechip athlete. Half of the young recruits believe 80 percent of the nation's major colleges are guilty.

Eight-four percent believe NCAA rules are too lenient, opening the door for scandals.

Almost half the athletes (47 percent) formed their opinions about recruiting by reading newspapers. Others learned by listening to high school and college coaches, other players and relatives.

Seven athletes said if a college offered a $10,000 summer job, a job for his father or a new car to renege on an oral commitment to another college, they would accept the offer.

"The temptation would be too great," said one.

Even before the 1984 season began, 11 players have been told by nationally ranked programs they are their No. 1 recruits at their positions. The list includes six Big Ten schools.

All but two of the athletes questioned said they believe recruiters aren't honest, just "good salesmen."

Thirteen said they were aware of athletes who had been "bought" by colleges.

Six said they could be "bought" by colleges. "If the money was big," said one. "If the price is right," said another.

Forty-two percent said they don't trust recruiters.[10]

In an effort to change attitudes like these and provide high school coaches with guidelines to better prepare their athletes to cope with the pressure of organized sports, Larry Hawkins, a former high school coach and director of the Institute for Athletics and Education of the University of Chicago, and Clarence Wordlaw Jr., a former basketball star with Iowa University, conceived a "Coaches Code" which I feel has considerable merit.

— I will prepare my youngsters well in the fundamentals of the game. They should, in a sense, know how to crawl before they walk.

— I will accept the reality that for them I am a pivotal figure and, therefore, I must strive to conduct myself in an exemplary fashion.

— I will impress upon my charges the importance of knowing the rules of the game and the spirit of fair play that is the basis of those rules.

— I will insist that players unwilling to participate in their planned academic experiences will not be welcome on the team.

— I will accept the responsibility for encouraging my players to seek out and use academic support systems when required.

— I will use competency as the sole basis of selection of game officials.

— I will accept the view that the relationship between coach and officials is not an adversary one. Furthermore, the officials' judgment calls are not all wrong and are not the only reasons I lose.

— I will shake hands with the officials and opposing coach before and after each contest.

— I will not physically or psychologically abuse my players.

— I will not allow an ill or injured player to return to competition until proper medical and/or parental clearance is received.

— I will have available at all practices and games a properly equipped first aid kit and a trained person to administer sound first aid procedures.

— I will collaborate with the parents of my players and use other community resources to improve my program.

—I will be in close and regular contact with counselors about the progress and plans for my players academic futures.

—I will constantly inquire and attempt to resolve the situations incumbent in the following questions:

a. What do I wish to be doing 10 years from now?

b. What will be my players' skill development and academic realities in 1, 2, 3, 4, and 5 years?

c. What is the relationship between athletic skill and academics?

d. How important is it for my players to have the ability to get along with other people?

e. Are my players able to see their opponents as human beings?

Ironically, the number of Black athletes performing for white colleges will decrease considerably by the year 1986. In its belated effort to improve the academic performance of athletes, the NCAA adopted at its 1983 annual convention in San Diego what is now called Proposition 48. This new ruling, which goes into effect in 1986, requires incoming student athletes to achieve a minimum combined 700 score on the scholastic Aptitude Test or a 15 score on the American Testing Programs's examination. The rule also sets a minimum 2.0 (on a 4.0 scale) grade point average in eleven academic high school courses, including at least three in English, two in mathematics, two in social science, and two in natural or physical science. Although these standards would appear to be in keeping with the level of academic achievement desirable for performing college work, it is unlikely many Black high school athletes will measure up to them. Among Black high school students, both athletes and non-athletes, the SAT has never been held high as an instrument for measuring a students' true potential to succeed in college.

Personally, I have mixed feelings about Proposition 48 because although I strongly support academic achievement, I, too, find the SAT not the best instrument for predicting what students will be successful in college. In my 25 years working with Black youth, I have seen many do poorly on the SAT, but yet excel as students. Nevertheless, there must be better monitoring of student athletes to ensure that they are properly educated to assume an occupation when they leave college. However, from a systemic point of view, this is essentially a problem which Black educators and the Black community must resolve. The majority of Black high school athletes still graduate from Black high schools, and it should be the responsibility of these institutions to properly educate Black youth. In Chapter 5 this problem was expounded on to describe what Black educators and the Black community must do to eradicate the educational disease that is maligning so many of our youth.

Because of the mesmerizing effect athletics have on Black youths, athletes have a great impact on youth as role models. Thousands of Black youths have literally grown up in the shadows of a Willie Mays, Jim Brown, Oscar Roberson or Sugar Ray Leonard. Their adulation for famous athletes far exceeds their admiration for outstanding Blacks in other fields with the possible exception of Black entertainers. Some youths are so engrossed with the athletic achievement of their athletic heroes that they virtually memorize all the statistics achieved by their idols. They can compute batting averages, field goal percentages and rushing yardage as though they were competing in a math exam. And in addition to retaining this information, they begin to emulate the life styles of their heroes. While hero worshipping is a normal phase in growing up, for youth with a Jock Strap Mentality, it becomes a fixation. As a result, there are more Black youth being influenced by a Magic Johnson than an Andrew Young, the former U.S. Ambassador and now Mayor of Atlanta. Many may respond to my example as being typical in view of the media hype given to Black athletes and the negative treatment it gives to most Black politicians. Granted, the idolization of Black athletes should be expected to exceed the admiration a Black youth will have for Black politicians when the priorities assigned to role models are made by white America. But herein lies the very problem; the power of white America to define our models. And to reinforce this power, white America often uses Black athletes as spokesmen for Black causes. Although some Black athletes may have large followings, they do not have an institutional base in the Black community which would provide them a legitimate platform to speak in behalf of Black people. And I have yet to see white super athletes like a Pete Rose or a Larry Byrd even be considered as spokesmen for whites.

Critics of Proposition 48, mostly Black educators and coaches, see this ruling as a device to weed out the number of Black high school athletes who would be eligible for scholarships; thereby nullifying their chance to obtain a college education. Presidents of Black colleges have especially been adamant in their disfavor of this ruling. Dr. Jesse Stone, President of Southern University, claims,"...it is a bad Proposition for young prospective athletes and Blacks in general." Another president of a Black college, Dr. Frederick Humphries of Tennessee State echoes Dr. Stone's sentiments. "We are opposed to Proposition 48 and what it means for the Blacks and other disadvantages youths in Division 1 of the NCAA and other smaller institutions." To further express their dissatisfaction with the ruling, some Black presidents have threatened to withdraw their schools from the NCAA. The supporters of this controversial ruling, mostly white, advocate that it is in the best interest of the student athlete and will help ensure that a greater number of athletes receive their diplomas.

It is my contention we need to reexamine the strong influence athletes have on our youth. This is not to imply Black athletes should not be role models, only that they should not be the only role models. Arthur Ashe, the retired tennis star and first Black male ever rated consistently among the world's top ten players, concurs with my feeling.

> In some respects, I suppose I am a role model for Black youngsters, even though until recently tennis was never the most popular sport around. I guess you wind up being a role model whether you like it or not. Sometimes I like it, sometimes I don't...It's all right for every American kid to emulate athletic heroes, but when you're 16, 17 or 18, it's time to switch your role models from athletics to something...a bit more relevant to what you're going to do with the rest of your life.[11]

If the Black community is to continue to tolerate the

obsession most Black youth have with athletics, it must begin to exercise some control over the manner in which athletics effect their behavior. Regardless of how appealing athletics are to Black youths, none of them provide the types of awareness and consciousness needed to combat racial oppression. There has never been an example in the annals of history of oppressed people freeing themselves from the yoke of oppression through athletics. Although healthy bodies are desirable, perceptive minds are more responsive to the challenges confronting Black people. White America is cognizant of this, and therefore, finds gratification in seeing so many of our Black youths flaunt their bodies around in quest for medals and lucrative contracts. Of course the other diversion favored by white America is to see Blacks sing and dance as though they were still rejoicing to the jubilees following our so-called emancipation. Athletics are, in fact, no more than another form of entertainment. They should not be taken seriously other than to provide a violent-oriented society with moments of thrills and breathtaking feats.

If Black youths are to develop their true potential, they must be inspired to emulate responsible Blacks in other fields and professions. It is the noticeable lack of interest in other fields and professions that has become a trademark of many Black youths. I'm not advocating that Black youths cease participating in athletics. Such a wish would be irresponsible and ignores the many values which athletics can foster. Values such as team work, individual competence and sportmanship are not to be frowned upon. When used properly they can be cornerstones to assist in the positive development of Black youth. But for Black youths to limit themselves only to the pursuit of athletic skills negate any opportunity they may have for other achievements. And to be saddled with a "Jock Strap Mentality" is not only self-defeating but a psychological barrier to the proper development of one's mind.

CHAPTER NINE

THE IMAGE MAKERS:
THE EFFECTS OF THE MEDIA
ON BLACK YOUTH

Directive images are shorthand
symbols of the ideals and aspirations of a culture. They tell people
who they are; they define roles and
apportion tasks. They are maps of
the territory and of the soul. They
define the paths, the obstacles,
the instruments, and the goals.
They project ideal images of the
ideal relationships between man
and man, between man and
woman, between man-woman-child.
They project, at least in embryo,
certain basic ideas about the accu-
mulation and investment of capital,
the role of the family and the transmission of values to the next
generation.

Lerone Bennett, Jr.
The Challenge of Blackness

"What's wrong with this picture? These words are the title to an ad produced by the Black Owned Communications Alliance. The ad was widely circulated in national magazines, and presented a picture that succinctly describes the effect images have on Black children. The picture is of a young Black boy dressed in a Superman costume. He is standing in front of a large mirror admiring himself. What he sees, however, is not his own Black image, but the image of the mythical hero he is emulating—a white adult male attired in the same Superman costume. Obviously what is wrong with this picture is the boy's self perception. That is, his inability to imagine his hero could be reflective of his color. Simply, he sees himself as white because that is the image Superman projects. Though we expect children, regardless of their race, to be influenced by images, the problem presented in this picture is one of proper identification. However, proper identification becomes a problem in itself when images are controlled by those who are bent on distorting a people's identity. For in a real sense, when you distort the images people relate to, you also distort, in part, the people themselves. This is not a pragmatic statement. On the contrary, it is a rational analysis of the function of images and their ability to impact a people's behavior.

One thing is clear. The image is built up as a result of all past experience of the possessor of the image. Part of the image is the history of the image itself. At one state the image, I suppose, consists of little else than an undifferentiated blur and movement. From the moment of birth if not before, there is a constant stream of messages entering the organism from the senses. At first, these may merely be indifferentiated lights and noises. As the child grows, however, they gradually become distinguished into people and objects. He begins to perceive himself as an object in the midst of a world of objects. The conscious image has begun. In infancy the world is a house and, perhaps, a few streets or a park. As the child grows his image of the world expands. He sees himself in a town, a country, on a planet. He finds himself in an increasingly complex web of personal relationships. Every time a message reaches him his image is likely to be changed in some degree by it, and as his image is changed his behavior patterns will be changed likewise.[1]

Using this quote as a reference, it can be presumed that a child's self concept and inner perceptions are molded by what he sees, hears and experiences. No doubt the experience of the boy in the ad contained few positive images of Black heroes and, as a result, his cumulative perception resulted in the idolization of white heroes. As tragic as this analysis is, it is common among Black youth. As images are accumulated during childhood, they are stored in a child's mind and eventually become fixed during adolescence. To what extent a youth incorporates a particular image is not based on its validity. On the contrary, the degree to which a youth is indoctrinated by an image is largely one of exposure. When the exposure is persistent and goes unchallenged, the youth will invariably assume the image is correct. It is this problem that has confused the minds of many Black youth, and contributes to what I call image perversion. Image perversion may be defined by the following two processes. First, it is the acculteration of an image that does not reflect the racial characteristics of the person who identifies with the image. This is the process which they boy in the ad has experienced. Second, it is the glamorization of an image that may or may not reflect the person's race, but conveys a distorted picture with which the person identifies. An example of the second is when Black youth identify with images that represent role models, either white or Black, which do not espouse or reenforce positive values and lifestyles. Both processes play an important role in the socialization of Black youth, and accounts for much of their confused and negative behavior. And the most distressing thing about them is that they are fostered by the manipulative doctrine of white racism.

Image perversion comes in many forms but its most notorious conduit is the *media*. Because of its tremendous impact, the media is the primary source for exposing Black youth to images. The other source of image perversion derives from racist and distorted histories that need to be rewritten to reflect the historical oppression of Black people which has contributed to the self-defeating lifestyles adopted over the years by many Black men and women. Many of these lifestyles, regardless of their coping abilities, have helped to establish patterns of living which have not served the liberating needs of Black people.

To appreciate the nature of black lifestyles, we must first understand that they have emerged from an environment which is atypical. This is to say that the black ghetcolony, because of its historical development, has been shaped by forces which were designed to create coping modes of behavior. As victims of a ruthless slave system, black people have had to develop unique coping postures to adapt to an environment that was insensitive to their survival. The environment that white America created for black people was predicated on fear, frustration, anxiety and death. It was an environment which disclaimed the humanity of people, and then attempted to make these same people dependent upon the inhumanity of their oppressor. And in such a dehumanizing environment, those who are its victims take out their frustrations and anxieties on members of their own group.[2]

In Home Is A Dirty Street, I elaborated on the various models that influence the lives of many Black youth. The most dominant models were the street man, hustler and the pimp. However, because these models have been shaped, to a large degree, by the oppressive nature of the ghetcolony, they have become reactionary and counterproductive in their values and lifestyles. In other words, they have developed coping postures which induce more pain and frustration than they combat. As a result, these reactionary lifestyle models become fixed links in the chain of mental and physical servitude that prevents Black people from breaking away from their oppression. Obviously, if Black youth are to ever escape this oppressive cycle, there must be a radical change in the images which help to shape their lives. Before we can discuss how to develop positive alternatives to this problem, we must first examine (or reexamine) how the media contributes to the shaping of these images.

The media is one of the most powerful and influential industries in America. Its capital assets are staggering, and there are but few areas in American life that it does not effect. Although its impact may have been less prior to the Industrial Revolution, it was still a major factor during the early colonial period. The printing of leaflets, pamphlets, books and newspapers was commonplace and helped to shape the thinking of the colonial populists. Indeed, the media played an important role in the perpetuation of American slavery.

When Africans were first brought to America as slaves, it was necessary for the institution of slavery to justify its existence. The media assisted in this justification by depicting slaves as heathens and savages who were better off in bondage than they were in their native land. This aberration created an inferior image of the slaves while reinforcing the alledged superiority of whites.

> For its full growth, intellectual and ideological racism required a body of 'scientific' and cultural thought which would give credence to the notion that the blacks were, for unalterable reasons of race, morally and intellectually inferior to whites, and, more importantly, it required a historical context which would make such an ideology seem necessary for the effective defense of Negro slavery or other forms of white supremacy.[3]

How these images affected the socialization of Black youth can best be analysed from the slave narratives discussed in Chapter One. Again, we must rely on this type of fragmented data because, as I have indicated, there existed little documentation of Black youth prior to the twentieth century. Most likely Black youth during this period did not consciously identify with these distorted images but, nevertheless, incorporated some of them in their lifestyles. As members of an oppressed group they had few options other than to adopt the lifestyles to which they were exposed. If their parents and other adult slaves mirrored some of these negative lifestyles, it is reasonable to assume that Black youths were influenced by them. To assume otherwise would be to suggest that their socialization was in a vacuum and oblivious to their environment. However this assumption violates every principle of human development and would best be ignored. Of course in today's conglomerate of media technology, it is easier to identify those factors which do directly influence the lifestyles of Black youth.

The Image Makers were intent on doing everything possible to destroy the slave's image of himself, and make him adopt a self image woven from the fabric of white racism. From this tainted fabric came the creation of the "noble savage," "contented slave," and the "tragic mulatto." These images became institutionalized and were to remain tatooed on the minds of whites throughout legalized slavery and Reconstruction.

In order to justify slavery in this place that W.E.B. DuBois once called 'the land of the thief and the home of the slave.' The mythmakers of that day were required to prove in their so-called literature that the slave was subhuman and underserving of human rights and sympathies. Hence, those rights endowed to man by his Creator did not apply to the slave. The first task was to prove to the white American the slave's inferiority. The second job was to prove to the slave that he deserved to be a slave. The mythmakers of that time tackled their jobs with great alacrity and so much success, so that two hundred years after the Declaration of Independence and more than a hundred years after the Emancipation Proclamation, humankind is still faced with the white problem all over this terrible wonderful earth. So that, considering also what happened to the courageous red men, it can be said, that historically, America has always been a country of killers, a land of nigger-makers.[4]

The literature referred to by John O. Killens produced a myriad of negative images of Black people which have been extracted from the celebrated works of noted white authors. During the heated battles between the abolitionists and the pro-slavers, literature was frequently used to politicize each group's position. While it should be obvious that the pro-slavery literature would be slanted toward demeaning Black people, many of the abolitionists writers contributed to his demeanor, as well.

Along with more grotesque specimens of black humanity, the novels of George Tucker, Gilmore Simms, James Kirke Paulding, John Pendleton Kennedy, and Nathaniel Beverly Tucker presented slaves who were, in the words of William R. Taylor, 'responsive to kindness, loyal affectionate, co-operative.' And, as Taylor has pointed out, proslavery novelists thus unwittingly opened the door to an antislavery use to the same stereotype.[5]

Even the most celebrated of the abolitionist novels, Harriet Beecher Stowe's *Uncle Tom's Cabin*, patronized Black people. Sterling A. Brown, the prolific dean of Black literature, made the following statement about this highly acclaimed work: "Uncle Tom, the pure Black, remains the paragon of Christian submissiveness."

The works of other so-called white liberal authors like Mark Twain and William Faulkner have also been promoted as being sensitive treatments of Black people. Yet, the "noble savage" image portrayed of Blacks by Twain in *Huckleberry Finn* and by Faulkner in *The Bear* only reaffirmed stereotypes of Black people that were fabricated by the institution of slavery. And the works of playwrights Eugene O'Neil and Marc Connelly were also tainted with images of benevolent racism. O'Neil's obsession with Black characters merely revealed his lack of understanding about Black people, and his own benevolent racism which he mistaken as liberalism. Similarly, in "Green Pastures," the paternalistic Connelly failed to evade the pitfall of ethnic misrepresentation which is typical of most works about Blacks written by whites.

The control of Black images by the Image Makers persisted with only minor opposition until the emergence of the Harlem Renaissance and the Marcus Garvey Black Nationalist Movement. While both movements advocated Black pride, their political ideologies and methodologies differ considerably. As these movements unfolded the images of Blacks changed dramatically from shuffling and driftless buffoons to proud and assertive individuals. Of the two movements, which for the most part functioned parallel to each other, Marcus Garvey's probably had the greatest impact on Black youths. This distinction is made because the Harlem Renaissance was primarily an intellectual movement which did not have a strong community-based propaganda component. Then, too, many of the Black writers, artists and poets who comprised this movement were supported by white patrons who controlled the marketing of their works.

On the other hand, the movement of Marcus Garvey was grassroot in its inception, development, and focus and, therefore, more impressionable and accessible to Black youths and the black masses.

Shrewdly exploiting the mood of pessimism, cynicism and despair, Marcus Moziah Garvey built the first mass movement among American Negroes. "Up You Mighty Race," he thundered, "you can accomplish what you will." Using as a slogan, "African for the Africans at home and abroad," Garvey preached the gospel of a united Africa under the rule of Black men. In the process, he recruited hundreds of thousands of black Americans in an extraordinary black nationalist movement. He gave his followers parades, uniforms and pageantry. He glorified everything black. God, the angels and Jesus were black, he said; and Satan and the imps were white.[6]

Despite the positive appeal of both these movements, the Image Makers were not to relinquish their control of Black images. In the 1900's the technology of the media had advanced considerably and its newest propaganda tool—the motion pictures—was beginning to merge as its prized instrument. Now the Image Makers had the means to saturate the nation with their arsenal of Black stereotypes.

In the early 1900's white moviemakers clung to the safe, non-threatening image of Blacks securely contained within the parimeters of the rural south and the myths of a loyal, happy, non-rebellious servant class. The Harlems of Urban America existed only as exotic playgrounds for weekend slumming by the rich. Blacks were suspended in a white world on the silver screen which suggested that black institutions such as the family and the church did not exist.[7]

One of the earliest and most popular cineramic desecration

of Black people was the arch-racist epic, "Birth of A Nation." This film of ante-bellum life used every imaginable stereotype to paint a picture of Black people which was to last for decades. From the images in this ominous film came a number of similar movies such as "Hearts in Dixie," "Way Down South," "Uncle Tom's Cabin," and the celebrated "Gone With the Wind." In film after film, the same Negro stereotypes appear—foolish and irresponsible citizen, the grinning bellhop or flapjack cook, the hymn singing church goer, the song and dance man, the devoted servant or contented slave, the barefoot watermelon eater, the corrupt politician, the hardened criminal, and the African savage.

This trend continued until the World War II years when Hollywood decided it was time to show Black people differently. Movies such as "Stormy Weather," "Cabin in the Sky," "Emperor Jones," and "Porgy and Bess" were all supposed to represent Hollywood's new treatment of Black characters. While these movies did, in a small way, vary from earlier stereotypes, they still lacked honest indept portrayals of Blacks and were made primarily to showcase the musical talents of Black people. Paul Robeson, Lena Horne, Ethel Waters, Bill Robinson, Rochester, Mantan Moreland, Steppin Fetchit, and Canada Lee were some of the Black performers who came out of this period. However, none of these performers except for Robeson and Lee, were offered any great challenge for dramatic acting, and it was obvious Hollywood only wanted to see Black people sing and dance on the screen. And when they were not singing and dancing, they were running from their own shadows or allowing their eyes to bulge out as though they had been removed from their sockets.

After World War II, the movie industry began to produce a few films which showed Black people with some human qualities. Pictures like "Intruder in the Dust, "Pinky," and "Home of the Brave" did depict Black people in roles which greatly differed from the stereotypes of earlier films. "Intruder in the Dust" was an effort to make a statement about the savage crime of lynching which was so prevalent in the South after Reconstruction. "Pinky," though using the familiar theme of the "tragic mulatto" did unsurface some of the myths about southern Blacks even if a white woman, Jeanne Crain, played the titled role. And "Home of the Brave" did have some sincere moments, although the final scene which showed James Edwards shedding crocodile tears over a white soldier who had earlier shown contempt for him left much to be desired.

In "The Defiant Ones", which gained Sidney Poitier an academy award nomination, a Black man was seen in another dramatic role. Although Poitier, who played an embittered escaped convict, did represent a new type of cinema image of the Black male, the final scene in which he sacrifices his freedom while trying to save the life of his white convict companion only reinforced the classic myth that Blacks harbor no malice toward their adversaries.

It was not until the urban rebellions of the sixties did the movie industry recognize the economic potential of the so-called Black movie. Thus, Hollywood tried to erase some of the racist taint from its record and set out to hire Black actors, Black writers, and Black directors. The result of this search ignited the production of new Black films which all claimed to be representative of the Black Experience. However, it quickly became evident that Hollywood was only interested in exploiting the hunger of Black people to see Black "super dudes" outwit and outfight the bad "white guys," regardless of how ridiculous and absurd the movies were. For some Black people watching these commercialized distortions of our lives were the only time they could see Black people gain victories over whites.

Ironically, the film which started the "blackploitation" movie trend was an independent film produced, written, directed, and starring Melvin Van Peeples. The opportunistic and gifted Van Peeples had earlier gained acclaim when he won a prize at the prestigious Cannes Film Festival for another film which he also wrote and directed called "Three Day Pass." However, whereas the latter film was simply a well-done document on the lives of three sailors over one week-end, Van Peeples' "Sweet Sweet Back, Bad Assss Song" was a crude sexual fantasy of a Black pimp's bizarre escapes with whores, unsavory characters, and eventually his escape after killing a white policeman.

Despite Van Peeples' claim that "Sweetback" delivered a

positive message to Black people, it became the center of controversy within the circles of Black militants and Black intellectuals. Huey Newton, chairman of the Black Panther Party, lauded the film for its alleged racism and political message to common Black people. On the other hand, Lerone Bennett wrote an incisive statement that criticized its overall value to Black people.

One ought to say this, one serves truth and liberation by saying this, but one also serves truth and liberation by saying that Sweet Sweetback, despite its acclaim and despite isolated moments of promise, is a trivial and tasteless negative classic: trivial and tasteless because of the banality of conception and execution; a negative classic, because it is an obligatory step for anyone who wants to go further and make the first black revolutionary film.[8]

The Image Makers quickly capitalized on the success of "Sweetback" and converted Chester Himes' detective novel, "Cotton Comes to Harlem" into a burlesque movie that became a box office smash. After "Cotton" came "Shaft," Hollywood's version of a Black James Bond and the proliferation of Blackploitation movies was becoming commonplace to the movie industry.

These movies did little to enhance the image of Black people. Despite their showcasing of "super Black heroics," which were far from being believable, most were saturated with violence, sex, and characters which even the worst ghetcolony would find intolerable. In addition, they were cheaply produced and dishonestly marketed as being representative of Black people. Black youths often found these "flicks" engaging and exciting. Even if they didn't believe what they saw, most were tantalized by the flambuoyant lifestyles which characterized the "brothers" and "sisters" who performed in these ridiculous films. In fact, the impact of these films on Black youths was not imaginary. In many Black communities, our youth could be seen sporting "Superfly" hair styles, wearing psychedelic colored clothing, and acting out the shenanigans of their newfound heroes and heroines. While some people may feel these images were improvements over the burlesque antics of a Mantan Moreland or Steppin Fetchit, they were, nonetheless, still distortions, and as such left much to be desired. In addition, the images of the Blackploitation movies were far more dangerous, because they projected an illusion that Black people could beat "whitey" by merely calling him a "mother—."

Following are a listing of the images produced by the movie industry prior to 1960 and during the Blackploitation period:

Pre 1960	Blackploitation Period
Contented Slave	Celebrated Hustler
Tragic Mulatto	Cool Pimp
Brute Negro	Sensuous Female
Wretched Freedman	Brute Negro
Sensuous Female	Black Stud
Black Stud	Stupid Militant
Happy Coon	Super Nigger
Timid Nigger	Suicidal Militant
Noble Slave	Bad Nigger
Bad Nigger	

As one can readily discern, the images that I have identified will never motivate our youth to achieve their true potential or make a notable contribution to the improvement of Black people. On the contrary, these warped images can only add to the confusion and misdirection which already plague the positive development of most of our Black youth.

The fledgling white motion picture industry during the twenties was not without its Black counterpart. Less publicized independent Black film makers were also using the media of film for portraying images of Black people.

Independent black cinema dates back to the World War I years when the medium of film and the fledgling film industry were both struggling for their survival. As a cinema which has existed within the shadow of Hollywood, an important basis of this black cinema is its development as a means of expression for the experiences of blacks as a subordinate cultural group.[9]

The independent Black film movement was begun by a Black actor, Noble M. Johnson, who started a film company in

Los Angeles in 1915. Other Black film pioneers were Johnson's brother, Swann Johnson, E. Toussaint and Oscar Micheaux, whom many consider the dean of black film makers. Though the films produced by early Black film makers were not always artistic gems, most did attempt to depict Blacks that greatly contrasted the racial stereotypes created by the Image Makers. Even though many of these roles were often fantasized, they, nonetheless, provided Blacks with images that were both romantic and heroic.

. . . for thousands of Black movie-goers in the 20's and 30's the image of Black good overcoming Black evil, of Black wealth and influence, of Black men protecting Black women was heroic. For many these films must have offered a glimpse into a fantasy world that reflected their own hidden dreams of heroes and villains. . . . Black audiences had been accustomed to a steady diet of the Black comic — always the butt of the joke, or Blacks singing or dancing their way to heaven in bit parts in white movies. Blacks saw themselves for the first time on film, cast in dramatic roles created by other Blacks.[10]

Black films such as Oscar Micheaux's "Homesteader" (1918), a saga of Black cowboys; the "Crimson Skull" (1921) which showcased the historic all-Black town of Boley, Oklahoma; and "Trooper K" (1916), a drama about a Black soldier were enthusiastically received by the Black community. No doubt these films left an impressionable image on those Black youth who were fortunate enough to see them.

Up until the forties, the movie industry was still the major media for marketing images. But after World War II, the media of TV began to challenge its supremacy. With the advancement of TV, the Image Makers could now market their images into almost every home in the nation. If the movie industry was the first mass molder of Black images, the television industry was the first to cast them in stone. Ironically, it was believed by many that TV would be more liberal toward Blacks. To some it was being hailed as the most significant invention, next to the automobile, of the 20th Century, and projected as a formidable force for educating the public and improving race relations.

In its earlier years, television held the prospect of a bright and appealing future for Americans. Decades before it became a popular reality in the late 1940's, many saw the emerging medium as a wellspring from which would flow great social, cultural, and intellectual benefits. Combining the other popular arts—radio, film, theater, literature—into a single, ultimate medium, TV seemed to be propelling the United States toward a new era in its democratic civilization.[11]

But like most promises which are associated with the American Dream, the TV industry was for Blacks no more than an extension of its contradictory and racist doctrine.

If the history of blacks in early television suggests that shows stressing authentic images failed to establish lasting success, the same cannot be said of those series and programs presenting Afro-Americans in caricatures drawn from a tradition of prejudice. The mass audience, and consequently sponsors and stations, looked more approvingly on the mammies, coons, and Uncle Toms of the past than they did on blacks seeking approval through non-stereotyped talents.[12]

With few exceptions, the TV industry reenforced every conceivable, stereotype of Blacks while only giving credibility to Black entertainers. So long as Blacks were seen dancing and singing the Image Makers felt secure. And why not? Black entertainers were endowed with immense talent and could be enjoyed by both whites and Blacks. But to showcase honest dramatic portrayals of Black people was intolerable. In fact, to do so would have been an indictment against racism itself. The promise of the TV industry to treat Blacks fair quickly succumbed to the racist standards established by white America. The proliferation of Black stereotypes on TV that increased during the fifties was spearheaded by the infamous Amos and Andy radio show. As one of America's favorite radio shows, the Image Makers felt it would be a natural for TV. But fearing that the white actors, Freedman Gasden and Charles Correll, who portrayed these buffoons on radio, would have less appeal on TV, the Image Makers began a national search to find Black replacements. The search was so intense and competitive that President Truman and General Eisenhower became talent scouts. Truman suggested that the actors might be found in the drama department of Texas State University, a Black school, and Eisenhower "recommended a (black) soldier whom he had known during the war." When the roles were finally cast with Alvin Childress as Amos and Spencer Williams as Andy, the minimal progress made by Blacks since Reconstruction was virtually wiped out. If my comments about this minstrel show appear exaggerated, it is only because those who may hold this view fail to understand the importance of images. Those who do understand their importance realize that putting Amos and Andy on TV was an affront to every Black person who had fought and died since slavery to gain self respect for Black people.

Despite protests from countless Black groups and a legal suit filed by the NAACP against the producers of this show (CBS), Amos and Andy was to taint the TV screen from 1951 to 1966 with some of the most outrageous and slanderous images yet seen. In its suit against CBS, the NAACP identified the following objectionable features of this maligned coon show.

It tends to strengthen the conclusion among uninformed and prejudiced people that Negroes are inferior, lazy, dumb and dishonest. Every character in this one and only show with an all-Negro cast is either a clown or a crook. Negro doctors are shown as quacks and thieves. Negro lawyers are shown as slippery cowards, ignorant of their profession and without ethics. Negro women are shown as cackling, screaming shrews, in big-mouth close-ups using street slang, just short of vulgarity. All Negroes are shown as dodging work of any kind. Millions of white Americans see this Amos 'n' Andy picture and think the entire race is the same.[13]

Today, the images of Amos and Andy and other Black stereotypes from early TV have been rekindled under the pretense of being less offensive to Blacks. The man largely responsible for this rejuvenation is Norman Lear, the godfather of ethnic comedy. However, Norman Lear added a new dimension to the old minstrel by making his shows appear to be humorous statements of social issues.

Unlike Amos 'n' Andy and Beulah, the comedies of the New Minstrelsy presented more than simple cliches. The element which, in the minds of Lear and Yorkin, redeemed their use of questionable images was the involvement of their series with pressing social issues. Unlike the facile plots of earlier situation comedies featuring Blacks, the story lines in Lear-Yorkin shows treated controversial national concerns. Where in American television had situation comedy ever handled such problems as venereal disease, abortion, alcoholism, rape, mastectomy and black bigotry toward whites? Yet, these were themes on episodes of Good Times, Maude, All In The Family, and Sanford and Son. Politics, poverty, welfare, black ambitions, sexual conduct and sexual preferences were projected now as legitimate topics for jokes and plots.[14]

Two of Lear's most popular shows were "Good Times" and "The Jeffersons." "Good Times," adapted from "Cooley High," a serious movie written by Eric Monte who lived in the Cabrini Green ghetcolony on Chicago's near north side, tried to show that living in public housing was not entirely an act of drudgery and despair. The show's feature character, J.J. Evans, played by Jimmy Walker, was no more than a clone of Willie Best or Steppin' Fetchit. Despite its obvious minstrel overtones, "Good Times" was not overly criticized by Blacks until the father, John Amos, was written out of the show. The exclusion of the father aroused dissent because it reenforced the racist myth that Black men lacked concern for their families. If my criticism of "Good Times" is skewed by my ideological bias, my indictment of "The Jeffersons" is based on common sense. As one of the longest running shows about Blacks, "The Jeffersons" has survived criticism from concerned Blacks and scripts that are so poorly conceived one would think they were written on the set during coffee breaks.

"The Jeffersons" is not only a caricature of Black life but uses Blacks to promote America's biggest lie—that its "dream" is color blind. Another Lear favorite among Blacks and whites is "Different Strokes." This writer views "Different Strokes" as being the most blatant of all Lear's so-called social comedies.

By exploiting another myth that Black people will not adopt Black children, "Different Strokes" conveys a picture of white benevolent racism and black dependency. Using the appeal of two talented Black youth, the whimsical Gary Coleman and the effervescent Todd Bridges, the series is predicated on the assumption that Black youth are better off being supervised by whites. As usual when the Image Makers have something going in their favor, they squeeze it for everything that is humanly possible. Using another Black child who came to national attention through the advertising media, ABC concocted a similar type theme, and recruited 12 year old Emmanual Lewis, the Burger King star, to be featured in "Webster." Like his counterpart, Gary Coleman, the engaging and talented Emmanual is adopted by a white couple after his parents are killed. What both shows, "Different Shows" and "Webster" are in fact saying is that Blacks have little interest in adopting Black children and are content on leaving their rearing to benevolent whites. The criticism I pose is not intended to deny there exists a need to increase adoption of Black children by Blacks, but to question the producer's motive for exploiting the problem. The Image Makers seem intent on depicting Black family life in a way that makes the Moynihan Report appear to be an objective analysis of Black people. Other Black-oriented shows such as "Sanford and Son" and "The White Shadow" do no more than reaffirm the racist view that Blacks can only deal with social problems in a comical context.

Besides its negative portrayal of most Black characters, TV's obsession with violence can also be seen as an undersirable influence. Black youth are already exposed to enough violence in their communities to need to be reminded of killings, muggings, and rapes during their leisure time hours.

One example of excessive violence on TV is the popular "A-Team" starring the Mohawk-appearing Mr. T. This show was cited by one critic as having 35 acts of violence per hour. What makes this show even more disturbing is that Mr. T, the non-verbal muscle man and jack-of-all-trades, has become a folk hero to many Black youth. Supporters of the personable Mr. T will argue that he is only acting out a prescribed role. This is true. And it was also true of Willie Best, Mantan Moreland, and

Steppin' Fetchit. In all fairness to Mr. T. he is known for his generous contributions to the Black community. But the image he projects on TV compromises its total impact.

I have attempted to give a brief overview of the role the media has played in the shaping of images for Black youth. As major communication resources, the movies and TV attract millions of Black youth daily. While I cannot provide statistics on the number of Black youth who regularly attend movies, the figure is undoubtedly extremely high. However, statistics on TV viewing are more accessible and reveal that 98% of all U.S. homes have television sets, with 49% owning more than one. The average TV viewing for youth has been estimated as being six hours a day. Other notable statistics show that two-thirds of the population rely on TV for its source of news, and half of the population ranks TV as its most reliable resource. These statistics clearly point out the need for Black parents to assiduously monitor the programs which are viewed by their children. And in light of the negative images which are on television and their social implications. Black parents must question if the tube contributes anything of real value toward the positive socialization of Black youth. Critics of my view of TV may ask what evidence do I have to support these conclusions? This is a fair question, and, therefore, I have extrapolated from a document, *Blacks and Television: A Review of the Research Literature*, summaries of studies done on television's relationship to and impact on Black people.

> Hinton, Seggar, Northcutt and Fontes alluded to what may be a trend: the portrayal of blacks as industrious, competent, and law-abiding, but usually in minor and insignificant roles. Seggar and Wheeler found that minorities were more likely to be concentrated in personal service occupations and to suffer from stereotyped images. This tendency to portray blacks in low-status occupations was also evidenced in a 1975 study by Northcutt, Seggar and Hinton.

> Research by Donager et al. indicates that it is instructive to examine character behavior as well as frequency of appearance of blacks on television. In their analysis of

character portrayals, they found that although blacks were featured more often in major roles, the roles still conveyed stereotypical messages. In a similar study, Reid found that racial stereotypes were the basis for character portrayals on television. For example, black females were projected as being especially low in achievement but high on dominance and nurturance. Seggar and Wheeler also found that blacks were likely to suffer from stereotyped images.

Banks found that black characters in all-black television casts were more likely to display stereotypical black characteristics than were black characters in integrated casts.

Roberts was concerned with the type of television programs in which blacks were portrayed. He examined black portrayal in a reality-type television program, the newscasts, and found that while blacks appeared in approximately one-fourth of the news segments, the majority of the time they were seen but not heard. This led him to conclude that in the context of world and national affairs the viewpoint of blacks is seldom expressed.

Fourth and fifth-graders in Greenberg's study were more likely than white children to say their favorite program was black oriented. But when Eastman and Liss tried to determine the ethnic background of preferred characters of blacks, white and Mexican-American elementary school children in Los Angeles and Ventura counties, the authors found that three-quarters of the black children preferred Anglo characters.

Very few studies in the empirical literature have specifically observed black children to determine if television has an influence on subsequent aggressive behavior in them. While there are too few studies to draw firm conclusions there is some evidence that black children do learn and perform aggressive and innocuous behaviors which they learn from televised models. Age, sex, race of model and whether or not the televised model received a reward or punishment have been found to have some influence on whether elementary and pre-school children imitated the models they observed on television.

In a study of fourth, sixth and eighth-graders in Detroit and San Jose, Greenberg and Atkin found that black youngsters actually watched television so they could learn how different people behave, talk, dress and look.

Why do black children watch commercials? In a study of high school students in Prince George County, Maryland it was found that black students were more likely than white students to watch television commercials for social utility, communicatory utility and vicarious consumption.

One interesting finding surfaced in a study of children in Hartford. When asking children to compare their family's happiness with the happiness of families in television commercials, the authors found that three-quarters of the black children in the inner city schools said their families were less happy than the families in the commercials.[15]

It can be concluded from the above studies that television, in its present form, has a negative impact on most Black youths. I choose to qualify this conclusion because I feel, if properly used, television could be a positive influence on young people. Gil Nobles, a long time Black television announcer shares my mixed prognosis.

I am convinced that TV is at least partly responsible for much of the negativism that today's youth is engaged in. I am also convinced that TV can redirect the behavior patterns of today's youth into positive channels.[16]

Before this is possible, however, television must undergo a radical reordering of its priorities and values. One way Black people may be able to make the television industry more accountable to them is by boycotting the products of those companies which sponsor shows that are denigrating to Blacks. Another way, and perhaps less tedious, is to simply refrain from watching certain shows. Television is first and foremost a commercial enterprise which is dependent upon advertisers for its survival. This is why TV polls are taken seriously by the networks, and the fight for prime time viewers is void of ethics. If a substantial number of people can be mobilized to either boycott a show's sponsor and/or not view it, there is a strong possibility it can affect the status of a show. This was done in the case of "Beulah Land", a show about the South before Reconstruction that was merely a clone of the stereotypic movies about Blacks which were so common during the thirties. "Beulah Land" was to be aired by but after a massive outcry from numerous Black organizations threatening boycotts and other forms of advocacy, the show was postponed and revisions made to the original script. When the show was finally televised, it had a limited audience and eventually was cancelled. Whether similar successes can be achieved with other negative shows about Blacks is questionable. However, the salient question is why do we as Black people tolerate and accept the trash that is heaped upon us without asserting greater demands on the TV industry. If we are to divert the tube from contaminating the minds of our youth, such advocacy is imperative. But we must not limit our advocacy to only denouncing the white media for exercising its true mission—the perpetuation of western propaganda. We must also begin to assume greater reponsibility for our own images, and their effect on Black youth. Image making is an art. But it is an art that is universal. As Black people we must use our talents to create images which are consistent with our needs as a people, and which are more representative of our aspirations. There is no excuse why we should allow the "Jeffersons," "Good Times," etc., and other burlesque shows to define who we are. Nor is there an excuse for us to pay the price of a five dollar ticket to see a movie where Black super dudes are performing ridiculous feats which would not appear believable in a three ring circus. We don't have to invent Black super heroes and heroines. We only have to resurrect the images of Queen Nzinga, Nat Turner, Harriet Tubman, Denmark Vessey, Toussaint O'Louverture, Mary McCloud Bethune and Malcolm X to exemplify heroics.

In the final analysis, however, those who will have the greatest influence on our youths are those who have daily contact with them. When Black youths are able to see, on a consistent basis, Black adults functioning as mature, assertive and proud individuals, they will be less prone to internalize negative images.

Black adults must regain and retain the heritage of values of our ancient and noble race. It is something that we seem to have lost during our journey from native Africa to this land. We must have a more solid credo to live by than a quest for dollars, and a stronger moral anchor to hold our lives steady. We must develop a sense of principle and commitment and then pass these values on to our young.[17]

As powerful as the media is, it cannot distort the image of a people whose living examples contradict the distortions. When Black adults exemplify the qualities which make for a strong and proud people, we will have strong and proud youth. Nothing the Image Makers can do will efface the actions of a people whose image is a true reflection of their culture and history. It is axiomatic that images which are imposed on a people can only survive with the submission of a people they are supposed to portray. Niggers are niggers not because white people call them niggers, but because they have accepted the images which typify niggers.

Black youths must be highly selective in their choice of images. Every selection they make is crucial, and binding on their behavior. The boy described at the beginning of this chapter has made his choice. Perhaps had he been exposed to a stronger Black presence, he would be able to see himself, at least, as a Black superman. However, true Black images should not be a reflection of white images. They must be a reflection of us as a people, past, present, and future. If we are to redirect the lives of Black youths, Black people need to be their own Image Makers.

CHAPTER TEN

PLANTING THE HARVEST:
A CONCEPTUAL MODEL FOR THE POSITIVE
DEVELOPMENT OF BLACK YOUTH

> When we can produce individuals
> emancipated from fears about
> themselves we will produce indi-
> viduals freed to feel with others
> and freed from the shackles of the
> old orders, —freed to conceive new
> orders and vigorous in the
> struggle to create them.
>
> Mary Ellen Goodman

The socialization of Kunta Kente consisted of an orderly process of maturation that prepared him for manhood. In traditional African societies this process is normally called the "Rites of Passage," although in his village of Juffure it was named Kafo. The Kafo began for boys at age five and consisted of three five year periods. Upon the completion of the first two periods, boys were then ready to commence their formal manhood training.

> Not a day passed that Kunta and his mother didn't feel both anxiety and joy at the approach of the next harvest, which would end with the taking away of the third Kafo—those boys between ten and fifteen rains (years) in age to a place far away from Juffure, to which they would return, after four moons, as men.[1]

Manhood training was considered to be the most important period in a youth's life, and every boy was expected to go through it if he was to achieve manhood. Kunta Kente's manhood training was designed to be in harmony with his environment, and therefore, it consisted of hunting, harvesting, physical fitness, and self defense. Girls, too, were expected to go through womanhood training which generally consisted of learning to do household chores, rearing children, caring for the body, and embellishing their female attributes. For example, in Achole, Uganda, a girl who had completed her womanhood training was considered to be mature and responsible.

> By this time an Acholi Village girl is highly accomplished by traditional standards. She does most of the cooking in the home now, doing everything without being told. She knows, or ought to know exactly what her duties are.[2]

In both manhood and womanhood training, sex instruction was taught to assist boys and girls during their puberty.

> The rite of circumcision of the boys and the excision of the girls is conducted in most puberty schools some time after initiation. The custom of a few societies, Ndembo, Nda, Nimm, by offering the parts taken away as sacrificial gifts to the gods of fertility, may suggest that in some parts of the West Coast it had once a phallic significance. Other

societies may use it as a primitive aid to cleanliness and as a preparation for the connubial state, an introduction to the full prerogatives of manhood and womanhood.[3]

All training was taught by a council of elders who also pass on to the youths those traditions and mores which were essential for the preservation of the village's culture. In this way, the community could be assured that its youth would be totally familiar with its culture, and, in turn, pass it on to future generations. What has been lacking, among other things, in the socialization of Black youth in America, has been the presence of an orderly process of maturation to prepare them for adulthood. This is not to say there is a complete absence of parental guidance among Black youth. Most parents do make a sincere effort to properly raise their children, often at great sacrifice. In all my years working with Black youth I cannot recall one situation where parents did not show this concern. But being sincere and showing concern are not enough if parents lack the knowledge and proper resources needed to raise Black youth. And because many Black families are burdened with other responsibilities—such as maintaining a job; coping with stress; and just trying to survive—they do not expend the necessary time or energy to monitor the socialization of their children. Many depend on other institutions to fill this void, but few of these institutions live up to their expectations. I have already elaborated on some of the reasons why institutions are ineffective; the most apparent ones being their own lack of preparation and commitment to respond to the real needs of Black youth. As a result of this vacuum, most Black youth become indoctrinated to the Pepsi Syndrome; the proliferation of a bias and trivial media; the over-glamorization of popular culture; and the racist propaganda that underlie American society. It is little wonder, then, that many Black youth become confused, embittered and demoralized. If we are to promote the positive development of Black youth, we must have a model that expressively addresses itself to their exceptional needs. By this I mean that the model must somehow penetrate the racist norms which permeate this society so Black youth will have the opportunity to maximize their development inspite of its adverse and debilitating influence. Furthermore, the model must engender values and attitudes which eradicate self-defeating behavior and replace them with liberating behavior.

In seeking a model that epitomizes these qualities, the one most representative for our purpose is exemplified in the principles of Afrocentricity. A model based on the principles of Afrocentricity provides us with the properties that best characterize the traditions and values needed to enhance the socialization of Black youth. In the formation of our Afrocentric Model, we will draw heavily from the research and writings of Dr. Molefi Kete Asante, Dr. Malauna Karenga, Dr. Wade Nobles, Haki Madhubuti, and Dr. Robert L. Williams. This is not to suggest that these scholars have an exclusive copyright on Afrocentricity, but an acknowledgement of the relevancy of their work to this commentary. In the development of our Afrocentric model, we are not making a claim that it is a replica of traditional African cultures. Such a claim would be irrational and ignores the influence of the highly technological society in which we live. Moreover, even if this were possible, I doubt if it would prepare our youth to function in harmony with their environment as was true of African youths who lived in traditional African societies. Nonetheless, we believe some of the principles that underlie traditional African societies can be applied to our model. These principles include the following:

1. Community Elders have a responsibility for helping to train youth to become responsible adults.

2. Youth cannot sufficiently teach themselves to become responsible adults.

3. The socialization of youth must be channeled through institutions that provide them with critical life-substaining support systems.

4. When the above three principles do not occur, we should not expect our youth to be totally responsible for their actions which are counter-productive to the welfare of the community.

Regardless of the discrepancies and contradictions we must contend with living in a society that is hostile toward us, we can adopt some of these principles in the socialization of our youth.

Although the concept of Afrocentricity is generically linked to the history and culture of African people, and has been expressed by many of its advocates over the years, it has been the work of Dr. Molefi Kete Asante that has crystalized it into a philosophical construct for implementation. In his scholarly treatment of Afrocentricity, Dr. Asante provides the foundation for its philosophy.

Afrocentricity is the centerpiece of human regeneration. To the degree that it is incorporated into the lives of the millions of Africans on the continent and in the Diaspora, it will become revolutionary. It is purposeful, giving a true sense of destiny based upon the facts of history and experience.[4]

Dr. Asante continues to state:

Afrocentricity takes a similar form once it is a fact in one's life; it is not linear, cannot be analyzed in a single line, and is inherently circular. I speak of it as a transforming agent in which all things that were old become new and a transformation of attitudes, beliefs, values and behavior results. It becomes everywhere sensed and is everywhere present. A new reality is invoked; a new vision is introduced. In fact, it is the first and only reality for African people; it is simply rediscovery. Our eyes become new or rather what we see becomes clearer.[5]

Dr. Asante's philosophy of Afrocentricity can then be applied to the concept of a Black Personality which Dr. Robert Williams has defined as WEUSI or the Collective Black Mind.

The Collective Black Mind is conceptually defined here as a corpus of philosophy, attitudes, preferences, values, beliefs and behavior—all of which are transmitted through Afrocentric space and woven with a strong spirituality. Thus the Collective Black Mind (CBM) will replace the individualistic (Non-collective) concept of personality; the Swahili term WEUSI will be used instead of the Eurocentric concept of "ego," "self," "me," "Negritude," etc.[6]

Dr. Williams further explains the structure of WEUSI by noting:

Conceptually, the WEUSI consists of three distinguishing qualitative features: (A) Blackness, (B) Collectiveness, and (C) Naturalness. In addition to these three features two quantitative attributes of *space* and *time* are central to developing the Collective Black Mind.[7]

The following figure provides a visual perception of Dr. William's' structure of WEUSI.

STRUCTURE OF THE WEUSI

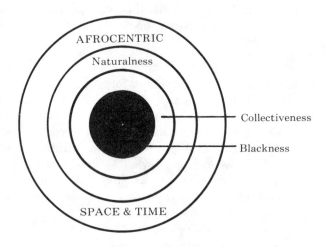

Afrocentricity also serves as the basis for Dr. Wade Nobles' explanation of the function of African philosophy in determining an African-concept and Black self-concept.

Consequently, the understanding of the psychology of Black people (more appropriately classified as Americanized Africans) must be African-based. Similarly, if we are to rid the literature of its scientific colonialistic tone, the proper understanding of Black self-concept must be based on African assumptions and must incorporate African-based analyses and conceptualizations. In this regard, we can clearly see the importance of understanding the African concept and its psychological basis for Black self-concept.[8]

Dr. Nobles uses the term "extended self" to explain African self-concept which he indicates is exemplified in the African world-view of WE instead of in the European World-View of I. These two contrasting world-views are shown in Nobles' Comparative World-View Schematic.

COMPARATIVE WORLD-VIEW SCHEMATIC

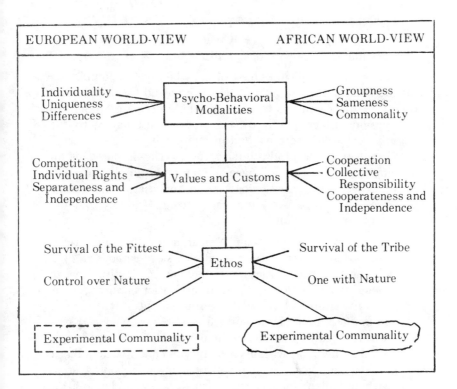

The differences in these two world-views are strikingly dramatic and corresponds to Dr. Asante's philosophy of Afrocentricity and Dr. Williams's structure of WEUSI. A key component to this model is the presence of a value system that provides Black youth with a collective commitment to the Black Community. Among his many contributions to the Black Community, Dr. Karenga has developed such a Black value system called the Nguzo Saba.

NGUZO SABA

Value	Meaning
Umoja	Unity
Kujichagulia	Self Determination
Ujima	Collective Work and Responsibility
Ujamaa	Cooperative Economics
Nia	Purpose
Kuumba	Creativity
Imani	Faith

These seven principles have already become the foundation for the value system of many Black people and Black organizations. By incorporating them into our Afrocentric Model, we will provide Black youth with a positive alternative to the negative values they often adopt in coping with a racist society.

Finally, Haki Madhubuti stresses the importance of developing an institutional base and a plan for implementation if we expect to re-create an African (or Black) mind in a predominantly European American setting. Madhubuti elaborates on this critical point:

No European can create an African mind. Only an African can do that. Yet, Africans cannot be created out of a vacuum. We need structure. Before you can institutionalize thoughts and actions, you need institutions and we say at IPE (Institute of Positive Education) institutions are built around a plan of action and we need to act in concert in a working plan in order to take the planet. You cannot reorder one mind without a plan; you cannot take a block without a plan; you cannot re-shape a school system without a plan; and to nationalize, organize, and mobilize a people you need—a plan.[9]

Obviously, if our model is to have a meaningful impact on Black youth, it must be operational. This however, has been one of our most serious shortcomings—the operationalization of theories and concepts conceived by our Black scholars. Parenthetically, this failure, over the years, has left many Black people with the impression that these theories and concepts are merely academic exercises which have no basis for implementation. So that our model (See Chart I) will not be conceived as being a sterile academic theory, we have designed a schematic to show its relationship to the principles of Afrocentricity and the resources needed for implementation.

Implementation of Model

We do not anticipate that our Afrocentric Rites of Passage Model will saturate the Black community over night. As much as we would like to see this happen, our logic is rationale enough to know this is only wishful thinking. There is a natural tendency on the part of most people to resist new concepts as being "impractical," "idealistic," and "pie in the sky." These people are more comfortable holding on to traditions. Because we have this perception, we are recommending that our model, first, be used as a pilot project with small, manageable groups. In this way, the model will have greater feasibility and application. We also suggest that whenever possible the model be implemented in an institution for greater exposure and credibility. The Black Independent Schools and the Black Churches are the most logical institutions for implementing the Afro-Centric Rites of Passage Model. In fact, most Black Independent Schools have already implemented some form of "Rites of Passage" programs, and there have also been examples in a few Black Churches. The Ebenezer Baptist Church in Atlanta, Georgia is one such church.

> Focusing on a younger age group, the leaders of Atlanta's Ebenezer Baptist Church have devised a unique "Rite of Passage" program which trains males, some of them five and six years old, in five categories, spiritual, cultural, economic, political, and personal development and initiates them into adulthood on their 13th birthday.[10]

In Norristown, Pennsylvania, Ebony cites another church that has adopted a "Rites of Passage" program. Reverend Frank T. Fair, the founder, initiated the program after visiting Africa with his son.

> When Reverend Fair and his son visited West Africa for six weeks in the summer of 1973, they learned about the

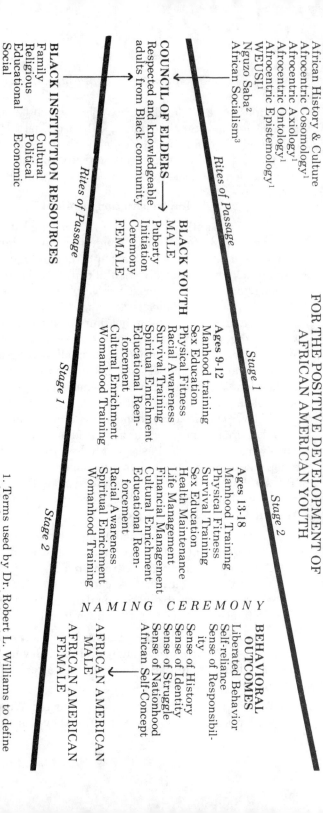

AFROCENTRIC RITES OF PASSAGE MODEL FOR THE POSITIVE DEVELOPMENT OF AFRICAN AMERICAN YOUTH

AFROCENTRIC PHILOSOPHY
African History & Culture
Afrocentric Cosmology[1]
Afrocentric Axiology[1]
Afrocentric Ontology[1]
Afrocentric Epistemology[1]
WEUSI[1]
Nguzo Saba[2]
African Socialism[3]

COUNCIL OF ELDERS →
Respected and knowledgeable adults from Black community

BLACK YOUTH
MALE
Puberty
Initiation
Ceremony
FEMALE

Rites of Passage

Stage 1

Ages 9-12
Manhood training
Physical Fitness
Sex Education
Racial Awareness
Survival Training
Spiritual Enrichment
Educational Reenforcement
Cultural Enrichment
Womanhood Training

Stage 2

Ages 13-18
Manhood Training
Physical Fitness
Survival Training
Sex Education
Health Maintenance
Life Management
Financial Management
Cultural Enrichment
Educational Reenforcement
Racial Awareness
Spiritual Enrichment
Womanhood Training

BEHAVIORAL OUTCOMES
Liberated Behavior
Self-reliance
Sense of Responsibility
Sense of History
Sense of Identity
Sense of Struggle
Sense of Nationhood
African Self-Concept

NAMING CEREMONY

AFRICAN AMERICAN MALE
AFRICAN AMERICAN FEMALE

BLACK INSTITUTION RESOURCES
Family   Cultural
Religious   Political
Educational   Economic
Social

STREET INSTITUTION

GHETCOLONY ←→ COLONIALISM
RACISM
CAPITALISM

Rites of Passage

Stage 1   *Stage 2*

Points of Conflict
⟶⟵

1. Terms used by Dr. Robert L. Williams to define his theory and model for the Collective Black Mind.
2. A value system created by Dr. Maulana Karenga
3. A term made popular by the late Julius Nyerere, president of Tanzania.

various ceremonies performed when African boys and girls "cross over" into the adult community.[11]

These examples are given to show that the "Black Church" can be responsive to the needs of Black youth when properly cultivated. There are also examples of "Rites of Passage" programs being implemented in other institutions. Paul Hill, Jr., the executive director of the East End Neighborhood House in Cleveland, Ohio has developed a comprehensive "Rite of Passage" program for males. The program is called SIMBA (Young Lions), and was commenced with 30 nine to twelve year old youths from single parent families. Other similar typed SIMBA programs are in Detroit and Los Angeles.

The critical factor in implementing the Afrocentric Rites of Passage Model is the creation of a Council of Elders. Those who sit on the Council of Elders in traditional African societies are usually highly respected adults who have a broad knowledge of the community's traditions and culture. The Council of Elders for our model should be comprised of similar adults. Despite what we are led to believe, there are adults who possess these qualities in almost every Black community. After a Council of Elders is formed, a chief is selected from the group and assigned the major responsibility for organizing the Rites of Passage program. The chief is also responsible for insuring that the other elders have a knowledge of Afrocentricity. To insure that all elders have this knowledge they should be required to read the following books:

—*Afrocentricity: The Theory of Social Change* by Molefi Kete Asante
—*Introduction to Black Studies* by Maulana Karenga
—*Kwanza: Origin, Concepts, Practice* by Maulana Karenga
—*From Plan to Planet* by Haki Madubuti
—*Kitabu: Beginning Concepts in Kawaida* by Maulana Karenga
—*Redemption of Africa and Black Religion* by St. Clair Drake
—*Destruction of Black Civilization* by Chancellor Williams

The major components for the Afrocentric Rites of Passage Model are taken from Dr. Robert Williams' definition of

Afrocentric philosophy.

Afrocentric Cosmology - African/Black Worldview that is the foundation for our thinking, beliefs, perceptions and values.

Afrocentric Axiology - A value system that serves as the foundation for what we believe and are willing to struggle for.

Afrocentric Ontology - Emphasizes our collective identity, collective struggle and collective destiny.

Afrocentric Epistemology - Stresses the importance of understanding our history, heritage and culture to acquire the knowledge we need to develop our fullest potential as a people and achieve liberation.

WEUSI - A theory for the development of a Collective Black Mind.

When the Council of Elders have digested these concepts they should be applied to the program components which comprise the workshops to be attended by the youths. Examples of this application are shown in Chart II.

The major program components to the Afrocentric Rites of Passage Model should include:

1. *Manhood and Womanhood Training*-to help youth understand and appreciate the responsibilities of manhood and womanhood so that they will develop proper attitudes and lifestyles consistent with these responsibilities.

2. *Sex Education*-to help youth cope successfully with the manifestations of puberty and learn to appreciate and respect their bodies so they will have a healthy attitude toward sex; learn how to regulate their sexual habits and be informed about "the facts of life."

3. *Physical Fitness and Self-Defense*-to teach youth to take care of their bodies, and help them to develop their physical attributes through the eating of proper foods and exercise. Also, to train youth in the fundamentals of self-defense so they will acquire the basic skills to protect themselves in situations that threaten their physical well being.

4. *Survival Training*-to train youth to survive in situations where basic life support systems are absent or limited, and to acquire basic skills in camping, farming, swimming, first-aid, and how to cope with catastrophic events.

5. *Health Maintenance and Hygiene*-to teach youth how to properly care for their bodies and emotional well being by developing health habits, values, and attitudes which discourages the use of drugs, alcohol, and other elements detrimental to one's health.

6. *Life Management and Values Clarification*-to teach youth how to organize and regulate their life styles to achieve maximum effectiveness, and to discern the difference between compulsive and rationale behavior. Also, to help youth set goals that are attainable and compatible with their abilities and skills.

7. *Cultural Enrichment*-to help youth appreciate and value the significance of African and African American culture as being the cornerstone for their socialization, and to develop their own creative talents to be supportive and consistent with the cultural energizers that best serve the liberating needs of African/Black people.

8. *Political Awareness*-to teach youth to understand that their lives are influenced and controlled by political decisions; and how to distinguish between those decisions that are in their interest and those which are not. Also, to help youth develop a worldview consciousness that is politically supportive and loyal to the needs and interest of African/Black people.

9. *Educational Reinforcement*-to help youth develop and maximize their intellectual capabilities to serve the needs and interest of African/Black people.

10. *Financial Management*-to acquaint youth with the basic principles of finance and money management so that they will better understand the system of capitalism, and how to use it in their's and the Black Community's best interest.

11. *Racial Awareness*-to teach youth the importance of ethnicity in helping them to realize their natural identity;

6. Life Management and Values Clarification	Afrocentric Axiology, Afrocentric Ontology and Afrocentric Epistemology WEUSI Nguzo Saba Value: Umjoa, Ujima, Nia, Kuumba and Imani	Teach youth to live within a framework of principles and values which reenforces a positive life style and provides clarity and direction.
7. Cultural Enrichment	Afrocentric Axiology, Afrocentric Ontology, Afrocentric Cosmology and Afrocentric Epistemology WEUSI Nguzo Saba Value: Kuumba	Help youth to gain personal and group satisfaction from exposure to and involvement in authentic African American and African Art Forms.
8. Political Awareness	Afrocentric Epistemology, Afrocentric Axiology WEUSI Nguzo Saba Value: Kujichagulia	Teach youth how political systems influence their environment.
9. Educational Re-enforcement	Afrocentric Cosmology, Afrocentric Axiology, Afrocentric Ontology, Afrocentric Epistemology WEUSI Nguzo Saba Value: Kujichagulia, Nia, Imani	Help youth to develop basic skills in reading.
10. Racial Awareness	Afrocentric Cosmology, Afrocentric Axiology, Afrocentric Epistemology WEUSI Nguzo Saba Value: Kujichagulia, Umoja, Ujima, Nia, Imani	Familiarize youth with people of African descent throughout the African Diaspora.
11. Financial Management	Afrocentric Axiology, Afrocentric Ontology WEUSI Nguzo Saba Value: Ujamaa, Kujichagulia	Help youth to share their funds, regardless of how small they are, for a common purpose.
12. Spiritual Enrichment	Afrocentric Cosmology, Afrocentric Axiology, Afrocentric Ontology, Afrocentric Epistemology WEUSI Nguzo Saba Value: All of them	Teach youth that Africa is the motherland of most world religions.

AFROCENTRIC RITES OF PASSAGE MODEL, FOR THE POSITIVE DEVELOPMENT OF AFRICAN AMERICAN YOUTH

PROGRAM COMPONENT	AFROCENTRIC PHILOSOPHY USED	TEACHING EXAMPLE OF PHILOSOPHY
1. Manhood and Womanhood Training	Afrocentric Cosmology, Afrocentric Axiology, Afrocentric Ontology, Afrocentric Epistemology WEUSI Nguzo Saba Value: Umoja, Ujima	Teach youth that sex roles are determined and defined by culture and group values which are in harmony with their environment.
2. Sex Education	Afrocentric Cosmology, Afrocentric Ontology, Afrocentric Epistemology and Afrocentric Axiology WEUSI Nguzo Saba Value: Nia, Creativity Kujichagulia	Teach youth that sex is a natural expression of one's physical and emotional well-being, but should be regulated and expressed through accepted group norms and values.
3. Physical Fitness and Self-Defense	Afrocentric Ontology, Afrocentric Axiology and Afrocentric Epistemology WEUSI Nguzo Saba Value: Kujichagulia, Umoja, Kuumba	Teach youth that their bodies should be properly cared for if they are to exercise control over their lives.
4. Survival Training	Afrocentric Epistemology, Afrocentric Ontology WEUSI Nguzo Saba Values: Umoja, Ujima	Teach youth how to maintain their physical well-being in life-threatening situations, and collectively work for the good and safety of the race.
5. Health Maintenance and Hygiene	Afrocentric Epistemology, Afrocentric Axiology WEUSI Nguzo Saba Value: Umoja, Kuumba, Kujichagulia	Teach youth to take proper care of their bodies and how to develop a life style that is conducive to good health.

establish meaningful relationship with others of African ancestry; develop pride in their heritage; and be committed and accountable to all African/Black people.

12. *Spiritual Enrichment*-to help youth acquire a spiritual affinity (not to conflict with their religious preference) with the universe that is based on moral principles which are uplifting, sacred, and binding on one's behavior.

The program components should be taught over an extended period so they can be properly digested and internalized by the youth. The elders have the responsibility for organizing and teaching these components in a manner that is stimulating but yet void of intellectual rhetoric. Upon completion of each program component, a youth should receive a certificate of recognition. Also when a youth has graduated from the program he/she should be encouraged to remain in the program to assist the elders in the instruction of younger youths.

The primary responsibilities for the Council of Elders are:

1. govern the implementation of the model

2. serve as extended family members to youth and their families.

3. be role models for youths

4. be advocates for the youth and their families

5. be the core instructors in the program

6. be knowledgeable of all resource material (see appendix)

To implement our Afrocentric Rites of Passage Model, the following features should be in place:

1. Council of Elders*

2. Minimum of 6 youths, ages 12-17

3. Support and cooperation of youths' parents

4. Resource material (see appendix)

5. A facility decorated in African motif

*Each Council should be of the gender it instructs.

Once these features are in place, the program should be structured around the following guidelines.

1. Weekly meetings
2. At least one elder for each six youth
3. Youth remain in program until 17 years of age
4. Graduating ceremonies for youths when they have successfully completed the program
5. Each youth is given an African name at graduation

The major objectives of the Afrocentric Rites of Passage are as follow:

1. to help a youth achieve a sense of his/her true identity and a feeling of belonging and commitment to the Black community and Diaspora.
2. to help a youth achieve a level of social maturity and awareness that will enable him/her to function in a racist society without engaging in self-defeating behavior.
3. to help a youth realize and achieve masculine and feminine roles that are satisfying, responsible, and consistent with acceptable cultural norms and values.
4. to help a youth develop a philosophy of life which allows him/her to function in a responsible and mature manner.
5. to help a youth to relate positive to his parents, peers, extended family, teachers, and elders.

It is important to note that the model we have presented is a conceptual construct and not a pragmatic solution founded on scientific conclusions. Also, as a conceptual model, it is subject to modification and improvement. Despite these precautions, however, we feel it has unlimited possibilities for the positive development of Black youth. Our primary goal in this commentary is to do just this—provide a conceptual model that can be applied to programs and institutions which serve Black youths. Such a model is needed to replace the traditional and archaic deficit models which have been institutionalized and imposed on Black youths. In the final analysis, the model we are advocating for the positive development of Black youth will have to be institutionalized on a massive scale if it is to have a significant impact on the millions of Black youth who live in America. This, indeed, is no small undertaking, and will demand a total commitment of the Black community to even begin to achieve this goal. I have no romantic illusion that such a task will be achieved if it is not approached collectively and with conviction, sacrifice, and relentless struggle. Even with these attributes, however, the task may appear to some to be beyond the capabilities and resources of the Black community. Yet, I firmly believe that if we fail to make an all out effort to reverse the present pattern of socialization for Black youth, our future as a people will continue to be clouded with hopelessness, despair, and defeat. The socialization of Black youth must be altered if we are to ever, again, emerge as a strong and independent people who have the potential for unlimited greatness.

It has been the intent of this commentary to define today's Black youth using the term that is generally accepted by most Black people. Thus the term *Black youth* was used because it indicates that the seeds for the harvest being advocated have not yet been planted. When these seeds are planted, nourished and reaped, they will produce an *African American* youth who has assimilated many African traditions during his/her Rites of Passage. It is at the completion of his/her Rites of Passage that a Black youth will be transformed into his true being and become an African American. For example, a Polish American uses this term to define his racial identity not only because he is of Polish ancestry, but because he identifies with and maintains some, if not all, of his Polish culture. This assimilation is also true of other ethnic groups, i.e., Italian American, Chinese American, etc. If a Black youth does not perceive him/herself as being of African ancestry, it is highly unlikely he/she will identify with an African self concept. The harvest we are advocating, however, will have a significant impact on the way today's Black youth perceive themselves—and that perception will bring about a greater recognition and appreciation of their African ancestry—thus an African self-concept. Chart III shows the socializing continuum that represents the transformation of African Youth to African American Youth.

In summary, we feel this model contains the seeds which are needed to sow a harvest that can develop a generation of Black youth whose potentials are fully developed and whose

SOCIALIZATION CONTINUUM FOR THE DEVELOPMENT OF AFRICAN AMERICAN YOUTH

Original Harvest	Contamination of Harvest		New Harvest
African Youth	**Slave Youth**	**Negro/Black Youth**	**African American Youth**
African self-concept	Damaged self-concept	Confused self-concept	African self-concept
cultural competence	cultural incompetence	cultural incompetence	cultural competence
obediant	low self-esteem	ambivalent behavior	high self-esteem
high self-esteem	passive behavior	depreciated character	positive behavior
positive behavior	depreciated character	adaptive behavior	transcendental character
group loyalty	adaptive behavior	confused group loyalty	self awareness
		median/low self-esteem	liberated behavior
		reactionary behavior	group loyalty
Rites of Passage	Disruption of Rites of Passage		Restoration of Rites of Passage

Copyright © 1985
Useni Eugene Perkins

values are reflective of the commitment and dedication which have become the trademarks for liberation movements throughout the world. If we are to ever escape the yoke of racism and oppression that have impaired our natural development since slavery, we must think seriously of developing and controlling our own models for change. This must be our mission—to ensure that our Black youth not only survive but rise to the heights they are capable of achieving.

 SOURCE NOTES

CHAPTER ONE

1. Edward Wilmot Blyden, *African Life and Customs* (London: African Publication Society, 1969), p.10.

2. Leon E. Clark, *Coming of Age In Africa: Continuity and Change* (New York: Frederick A. Praeger Publishers, 1969) p. 12.

3. Paul Bohannan, *Africa and Africans* (New York: Natural History Press, 1964), p. 170.

4. Francis Dow, *Slave, Ships and Slavery* (New York: Dover Publications, Inc. 1970), p. xxii.

5. Alex Haley, *Roots,* (New York: Doubleday, 1976), p. 183.

6. Lerohe Bennett, Jr., *Before the Mayflower: A History of Black Americans* (Chicago: Johnson Publishing Co., Inc., 1961), p. 70.

7. John Hope Franklin, *From Slavery To Freedom* (New York: Alfred A. Knopf, 1947), p. 206.

8. A. Leon Higginbotham, Jr., *In the Matter of Color* (New York: Oxford University Press, 1978), p. 44.

9. Ibid., p. 26.

10. Bennett, op.cit., p.

11. Ibid., p. 73.

12. La Frances Rogers-Rose, "The Black Woman: A Historical Overview," *The Black Woman* (Beverly Hills: Sage Publications, 1980), p. 19.

13. Margaret Walker, *Jubilee* (Boston: Houghton Mufflin Co., 1966), p. 94.

14. Herbert G. Gutman, *The Black Family in Slavery and Freedom* (New York: Vintage Books, 1977), p. 263.

15. Ibid., p. 263.

16. Ibid., p. 263.

17. Arna Bontemps, *Great Slave Narratives* (Boston: Beacon Press, 1969), p. 28.

18. Ibid., p. 34.

19. Ibid., p. 207.

20. Frederick Douglass, *My Bondage and My Freedom* (New York: Arno Press, 1969), p. 126.

21. _____, *Life and Times of Frederick Douglass* (New York: Collier Books, 1962), p. 126.

22. Booker T. Washington, "Up From Slavery," *Growing Up Black* (ed.) Jay Davis, (New York: William Morrow & Co., 1968), p. 114.

23. Ibid., p. 114.

24. Ibid., 117.

25. Ibid., 126.

26. Erlene Stetson, "Studying Slavery: Some Literary and Pedagogical Considerations on the Black Female Slave," *But Some Of Us Are Brave* (ed.) Gloria T. Hull, Patricia Bell Scott and Barbara Smith, (New York: Feminist Press, 1982), p. 62.

27. Linda Brent, *Incidents in the Life of a Slave Girl* (New York: Harcourt Brace Jovanovich Publishers), p. 5.

28. Ibid., p. 6.

29. Ibid., p. 6.

30. Ibid., p. 26.

31. Ibid., p. 26.

32. Ibid., p. 208.

33. Leslie A. White, *The Science of Culture: A Study of Man and Civilization*, (New York: Farrar, Straus and Giroux, 1969) p. 84.

CHAPTER TWO

1. Coming of Age in the Ghetto, "The American Underclass," *Time Magazine*, p. 76.

2. *Time Magazine*, August 29, 1977, p. 15.

3. Douglas G. Glasgow, *The Black Underclass*, (New York: Vintage Books, p. 11.

4. Ibid., p. 3.

5. *Time Magazine*, 1977, p. 8.

6. Hilda Taba and Deborah Elkins, *Teaching Strategies For the Culturally Disadvantaged*, (Chicago: Rand McNally & Co., 1966), p. 8.

7. William Ryan, *Blaming the Victim*, (New York: Random House, 1971), p. 6.

8. Samuel F. Yette, *The Choice: The Issue of Black Survival in America*, (New York: G.P. Putnam's Sons, 1971), p. 81.

9. Frantz Fanon, *Black Skin, White Masks*, (New York: Grove Press, Inc.), p. 16.

10. Ibid., p. 143.

11. Melville J. Herksovits, *The Myth of the Negro Past*, (Boston: Beacon Press, 1958), p. 187.

12. Ibid., p. 9.

13. Wade W. Nobles, "African Philosophy: Foundations for Black Psychology," *Black Psychology* (ed.) Reginald L. Jones, (New York: Harper & Row, 1972), p. 30.

14. Leslie A. White *The Science of Culture* (New York: Farrar Straus & Giroux, 1949), p. 131.

15. Ibid., p. 126.

16. Ibid., p. 127.

17. Robert L. Williams, *The Collective Black Mind: An Afro-Centric Theory of Black Personality* (Unpublished manscript) p. 56.

18. Ibid., p. 64.

19. Na'im Akbar, "Cultural Expressions of the African American Child," *Black Child Journal*, Vol. 2, No. 2, 1981, p. 7.

20. Ibid., p. 8-12.

21. David R. Burgest, "Afrocircular Child in the Eurolinear Society," *Black Child Journal*, Vol. 2, No. 1, 1980, o. 16.

22. Ibid., p. 17.

23. Janice R. Hale, *Black Children: Their Roots, Culture and Learning Styles*, (Brigham Young University Press, 1982), p. 15-18.

24. Vincent Harding

25. Lerone Bennett

26. Frederick Douglass

CHAPTER THREE

1. Ira De A. Reid, "The Socialization of the Negro in the American Social Order," *Journal of Negro Education* Vol. XIX (Washington, D.C., 1950), p. 27.

2. Leon W. Chestang, "Character Development in a Hostile Environment" (Self-published document, 1972), p. 2.

3. Ibid., p. 4.

4. Ibid., p. 5.

5. Thomas J. Edwards, "Looking Back on Growing Up Black," *Psychology and the Black Experience*, ed. Roderick W. Pugh (Monterey, California: Brooks/Cole Publishing Co., 1972), p. 65.

6. Frances Cress Welsing, "Black Value Systems and Strategies," *The Survival of Black Children and Youth*, ed. Jay Chunn (Washington, D.C.: Nuclossus and Science Publishing Co., 1974), p. 67.

7. Ibid., p. 69.

8. Victoria Secunda, *By Youth Possessed* (New York: Bobbs-Merrill Company, Inc., 1984), p. 41.

9. Erik H. Erikson, *Childhood and Society* (New York: W.W. Norton & Co., 1950), p. 306.

10. Louise J. Kaplan, Adolescence: *The Farewell to Childhood* (New York: Simon and Schuster, 1984), p. 36.

11. Hollis R. Lynch, *Black Urban Condition* (New York: Thomas Y. Crowell Company, 1973), p. 48.

12. Claude Brown, *Manchild In The Promised Land* (New York: Macmillan Company, 1965), p. 256.

13. _____, "Return To Harlem," *Tribune*, 23 September 1984, p. 4.

14. Robert Rosenthal et al., *Different Strokes: Pathways to Maturity in the Boston Ghetto* (Boulden, Colorado: Westview Press, 1976), p. 56.

15. Douglas G. Glasgow, *The Black Underclass* (New York: Vintage Books, 1981), p. 89.

16. Joyce A. Ladner, *Tomorrow's Tomorrow* (New York: Doubleday & Co., Inc., 1971), p. 125.

17. David Elkind, *All Grown Up and No Place To Go: Teenagers In Crisis* (Reading, Massachusetts: Addison-Wesley Publishing Company, 1984), p. 45.

18. Robert Staples, *Black Masculinity: The Black Male's Role in American Society* (San Francisco, California: Black Scholar Press, 1982), p. 79.

19. Max Sugar, *Female Adolescent Development* (New York: Brunner Mazel, 1979), p. 265.

20. Patricia Y. Miller and William Simon, "Development of Sexuality in Adolescents," *Handbook of Adolescent Psychology* ed. Joseph Adelsen (New York: John Wiley & Sons, 1980), p. 392.

21. Alfred B. Pasteur and Ivory L. Toldson, *Roots of Soul*

22. Lerone Bennett, Jr., "The Lost Found Generation," *Ebony*, August, 1978, p. 37.

CHAPTER FOUR

1. Ralph Ellison, "An American Dilemma: A Review," *The Death of White Sociology* ed. Joyce Ladner (New York: Random House, 1973), p. 83.

2. Ibid., p. 83.

3. Albert Murray, "White Norms, Black Deviation," *The Death of White Society* ed. Joyce Ladner (New York: Random House, 1973), p. 100.

4. Robert Staples, "What Is Black Sociology?" *Toward A Sociology of Black Liberation* ed. Joyce Ladner (New York: Random House, 1973), p. 164.

5. Eugene Perkins, *Home Is A Dirty Street: The Social Oppression of Black Children* (Chicago: Third World Press, 1975), p. 26.

6. Ibid., p. 26.

7. Ibid., p. 3.

CHAPTER FIVE

1. "A Nation At Risk," *The National Commission on Excellence in Education* (Washington, D.C.: U.S. Department of Education, 1983), p. 5.

2. Ibid., p. 7.

3. Hugh J. Scott, *The Black School Superintendent: Messiah or Scapegoat?* (Washington, D.C.: Howard University Press, 1980), p. 21.

4. Hannibal Tiries Afrik, *Education for Self Reliance, Idealism To Reality: An Analysis of the Independent Black School Movement* (Stanford, California: CIBI Publication), p. 15.

5. Faustine Childress Jones, *A Traditional Model of Educational Excellence* (Washington, D.C.: Howard University Press, 1981), p. 3.

6. Ronald R. Edmonds, "Programs of School Improvement: An Overview."

7. Ibid., p. 352.

8. Meyer Weinberg, *A Chance To Learn, A History of Race and Education in the United States* (New York: Cambridge University Press, 1977), p. 13.

9. Ibid., p. 352.

10. Ibid., p. 32.

11. Maurice Gibbons, *The New Secondary Education: A Phi Delta Kappa Task Force Report* (Bloomington, Indiana: Phi Delta Kappa, Inc., 1976), p. 46.

12. Black School Superintendent, p. 168-170.

13. Vernon Jerrett, *Chicago Sun-Times*, 22 April 1984, p. 18.

14. Livinus A. Ukachi, *Urban Education, Problems and Issues* (New York: Vantage Press, 1980), p. 75.

15. Eugene Perkins, *Home Is A Dirty Street: The Social Oppression of Black Children* (Children: Third World Press, 1975), p. 98.

16. Paulo Freire, *Pedagogy of the Oppressed* (New York: The Seabury Press, 1973), p. 31.

17. Ibid., p. 36.

18. Carter G. Woodson, *Miseducation of the Negro*, p. xxxiii.

19. Ibid., p. xxxi.

20. William E. Sedlacek and Glenwood C. Brooks, Jr., *Racism In American Education: A Model for Change* (Chicago: Nelson-Hall, 1976), p. 45.

21. Lerone Bennett, Jr., *Before the Mayflower* (Chicago: Johnson Publishing Co., Inc., 1961), p. 256.

22. Ibid., p. 257.

CHAPTER SIX

1. Joyce A. Ladner, *Tomorrow's Tomorrow* (New York: Doubleday & Co., Inc., 1971), p. 116.

2. Toni Cade, *The Black Woman* (New York: Mentor Book, 1970), p. 163.

3. Louise Meriwether, "Teenage Pregnancy," *Essence*, April, 1984, p. 96.

4. Frances Cress Welsing, "When Birth Is A Tragedy-Black Teenage Reproduction" (self-published essay), p. 3.

5. Ibid., p. 3.

6. Robert Staples, *Black Masculinity* (San Francisco: Black Scholar Press, 1982), p. 81.

7. Joyce Ladner, *Tomorrow's Tomorrow* (New York: Doubleday & Co., Inc., 1981), p. 199.

8. Ibid., p. 199.

9. John R. Porter, *Dating Habits of Young Black Americans* (Dubuque, Iowa: Kendall/Hunt Publishing Co., 1979), p. 64.

10. Ibid., p. 66

11. Ladner, op.cit., p.

12. Leo E. Hendricks,

13. Ibid., p.

14. Ibid., p.

15. Brochure of Sisterhood of Black Single Mothers, Inc., Brooklyn, New York.

16. Frances Cress Welsing, op. cit., p. 1.

17. Ibid., p. 3.

CHAPTER SEVEN

1. Harry Edwards, *The Struggle That Must Be* (New York: McMillan Co., Inc., 1980), p. 78.

2. Ibid., p. 259.

3. Martin Binken et al., *Blacks and the Military* (Washington, D.C.: Brookings Institution, 1982), p. 11.

4. Ellen Gibson Wilson, *The Loyal Blacks* (New York: G.P. Putnam's Sons, 1976), p. 22.

5. _____, *Smoked Yankees and the Struggle For Empire* (Chicago: University of Illinois Press, 1971), p. 21.

6. Jean Gillette, "Buffalo Soldiers: Horsemen of the West," *Mainstream America* (Los Angeles: Herrill Company, Inc. 1984), p. 50.

7. Jesse J. Johnson, *Black Women In the Armed Forces* (Hampton, Virginia: Hampton Institute, 1974), p. 1.

8. Binken, op. cit., p. 30.

9. Wallace Terry Bloods, p. 6.

10. Ibid., p. 25.

11. Ibid., p. 35.

12. Ibid., p. 55.

13. Ibid., p. 64.

14. Ibid., p. 142.

15. Ibid., p. 204.

16. Binkin, op. cit., p. 40.

17. Ibid., p. 53.

18. Ibid., p. 52.

19. Ibid., p. 67.

20. Jean Wiley, "Inside Grenada," *Essence*, October, 1984, p. 148.

21. Ibid., p. 156.

CHAPTER EIGHT

1. Timothy J. Curry and Robert M. Jiobu, *Sports, A Social Perspective* (New Jersey: Prentice-Hall, Inc. 1984), p. 92.

2. Ibid., p. 101.

3. Ibid., p. 101.

4. John C. Gaston, "The Destruction of the Young Black Male: The Impact of Popular Culture and Organized Sports" (Unpublished paper, 1983), p. 3.

5. David Wolf, *FOUL!* (New York: Hold, Rinehart and Winston, 1972), p. 21.

6. Ibid., p. 21.

7. Kareem Abdul-Jabbar and Peter Knobler, *Giant Steps* (New York: Bantam Books, 1983), p. 76.

8. Pete Axthelm, *The City Game* (New York: Harper's Magazine Press Book, 1970), p. ix.

9. Harry Edwards, *The Struggle That Must Be* (New York: McMillan Co., Inc., 1980), p. 16.

10. *Chicago Sun-Times*, August 9, 1984.

11. Chicago Defender, May 18, 1984.

CHAPTER NINE

1. Kenneth E. Boulding, *The Image* (Ann Arbor: University of Michigan Press: 1971), p. 6.

2. Eugene Perkins, *Home Is A Dirty Street: The Social Oppression of Black Children* (Chicago: Third World Press, 1976), p. 75.

3. George Fredrickson, *The Black Image in the White Mind* (New York: Harper and Row, 1971), p. 2.

4. John O. Killens, "The Image of Black Folk in American Literature," speech published by Howard University Institute for the Arts and the Humanities at the National Conference of Afro-American Writers, November 8, 1974.

5. Fredrickson, op. cit., p. 102.

6. Lerone Bennett, Jr., *Before the Mayflower* (Chicago: Johnson Publishing Co., 1969), p. 296.

7. Pearl Bowser, "Sexual Imagery and the Black Woman in American Cinema," *Black Cinema Aesthetics* ed. Gladstone L. Yearwood (Athens, Ohio: Ohio University Center for Afro-American Studies, 1982), p. 41.

8. Lerone Bennett, *The Challenge of Blackness* (Chicago: Johnson Publishing Co., 1972), p. 275.

9. Gladstone L. Yearwood, "Introduction: Issues in Independent Black Filmmaking," Black Cinema Aesthetics ed. Gladstone L. Yearwood (Athens, Ohio: Ohio University, 1982), p. 9.

10. Pearl Bowser, "History Lesson: The Boom is Really on Echo in Black Creation," *Quarterly Review of Black Arts and Letters*, 1973, p. 33.

11. J. Fred MacDonald, *Black and White TV* (Chicago: Nelson Hall Publishers, 1983), p. xiii.

12. Ibid., p. 22.

13. Ibid., p. 28.

14. Ibid., p. 177.

15. *Blacks and Television: A Review of the Research Literature*, p. 106-107, 111, 114-117.

16. Gil Noble, *Black As the Color of my TV Tube* (Secaucus, New Jersey: Lyle Stuart, Inc., 1981), p. 186.

17. Ibid., p. 183.

CHAPTER TEN

1. Alex Haley, *Roots* (New York: Doubleday & Co., 1976), p. 73.

2. Anna Apoko, "Growing Up in Acoli," *Coming of Age in Africa* ed. Leon E. Clark (New York: Frederick A. Praeger, 1969), p. 27.

3. F.W. Butt-Thompson, *West African Secret Societies* (Westport, Connecticut: Negro University Press, 1929), p. 122.

4. Molefi Kete Asante, *Afrocentricity: The Theory of Social Change* (Buffalo, New York: Amulefi Publishing Co., 1980), p. 4.

5. Ibid., p. 4.

6. Robert L. Williams, *The Collective Black Mind: An Afro-Centric Theory of Black Personality* (unpublished manuscript), p. 28.

7. Ibid., p. 31.

8. Wade W. Nobles, "Extended Self: Rethinking the So-called Negro Self Concept," *Black Children Just Keep On Growing* ed. Madeline Coleman (Washington, D.C.: Black Child Development Institute, Inc., 1977), p. 162.

9. Haki Madhubuti, From *Plan to Planet* (Chicago: Broadside Press, 1973), p. 45.

10. *Ebony*, February, 1985, p. 66.

11. ————, December, 1974, p. 83.

◥◣◥◣◥◣◥◣ BIBLIOGRAPHY ◥◣◥◣◥◣◥◣

1. Frederick Douglass, "The Meaning of July Fourth for the Negro," *The Voice of Black America* ed. Philip Foner (New York: Simon and Schuster, 1972).

2. W.E. Burhardt DuBois, *The Souls of Black Folk* (New York: Fawcett Publishers, 1967).

3. Claude McKay, "If We Must Die," *American Negro Poetry* ed. Arna Bontemps (New York: Hill and Wang, 1974).

4. Kenneth B. Clark, *Dark Ghetto, Dilemmas of Social Power* (New York: Harper & Row, 1965).

5. Howard Thurman, *The Luminous Darkness* (New York: Harper & Row, 1965).

6. Useni Eugene Perkins, *Home Is A Dirty Street* (Chicago: Third World Press, 1975).

7. Ayi Kwei Armah, *Two Thousand Seasons* (Chicago: Third World Press, 1979).

◥◥◥◥◥◥◥◥ APPENDIX ◥◥◥◥◥◥◥◥

I. Required Reading for Rites of Passage Model
II. Resource Books for Rites of Passage Model
III. Organizational Resources for Black Youth
IV. Educational Resources for Black Youth
V. Resource Books on Black Youth
VI. Key Characteristics of Black Youth

I. Required Reading for Rites of Passage Module

Up From Slavery, Booker T. Washington
My Bondage and My Freedom, Frederick Douglass
Roots, Alex Haley
Autobiography of Malcolm X, Alex Haley
Manchild in the Promised Land, Claude Brown
Black Boy, Richard Wright
Harriet Tubman, The Moses of Her People, Sarah Bradford
Autobiography of Ida B. Wells, Alfreda M. Duster
Angela Davis, Angela Davis

The above books are required reading for the Rites of Passage Module. They have been selected because each provides a graphic description of how some Black youths have been able to cope with oppression. In addition, each book describes the author's own "Rites of Passage" in reaching adulthood. There should be no time restraint placed on completing a book and each book should be discussed in small groups led by an elder. Upon completion of each book, a test should be given to see if the participant has learned the basic principles and values associated with the book. Although other questions may be asked, it is important to include the following:

1. What values were learned from reading the book?

2. Who were the major influences on the lives of the hero or heroine?

3. How did the hero or heroine deal with oppression?

4. Who were the antagonists in the book?

5. Identify positive and negative characteristics of the hero or heroine.

When a youth has successfully completed each book, he/she should be given the following certificate:

Rites of Passage Required Reading
Certificate

This certificate that _____ has successfully read the required books for his/her Rites of Passage. The knowledge learned in these books will serve as a valuable resource in helping _____ achieve adulthood.

_____   _____
Date   Council of Elders

II. Resource Books for Rites of Passage Module

The Poetry of the Negro, Langston Hughest & Arna Bontemps
Before the Mayflower, Lerone Bennett
Challenge of Blackness, Lerone Bennett
Destruction of Black Civilization, Chancellor Williams
The World and Africa, W.E.B. DuBois
Souls of Black Folk, W.E.B. DuBois
The Choice, Sam Yette
Mis-Education of the Negro, Carter G. Woodson
Paul Robeson: The Great Forerunner, Editors of Freedomway
Here I Stand, Paul Robeson
From Plan to Planet, Haki Madhubuti
Black Women, Feminism, And Black Liberation: Which Way?, Vivian G. Gordon

These books are not required reading but youths should be encouraged to read them, and refer to them as resources throughout their Rites of Passage.

III. Organization Resources for Black Children & Youths

The following resources are listed to assist those who are interested in the positive development of Black youths. It should be noted, however, that the author has not had the opportunity to screen the services of all these organizations, but is recommending them because they appear to be responsive to the needs of Black youths. Also, this list is by no means intended to be representative of all the organizations which serve Black youths.

Homes for Black Children
Family and Children Services
929 L Street N.W.
Washington, D.C. 20001

COAC Black Child Advocacy Program
875 Avenue of the Americas
New York, New York 10001

Advocates for Black Children
2822 55th Avenue
Oakland, California 94605

National Black Child Development Institute
1463 Rhode Island Avenue N.W.
Washington, D.C.

Alpha Phi Alpha
National Headquarters
4432 Martin Luther King Drive
(Project ALPHA Program for Unwed Teenage Fathers)
Chicago, Illinois 60653

DuSable Museum of African American History
740 East 56th Place
Chicago, Illinois 60637

National Alliance of Black School Educators
1118 9th Street N.W.
Washington, D.C. 20001

National Council of Negro Women
1819 H Street N.W. Suite 900
Washington, D.C. 20006

Children's Defense Fund
122 C Street N.W. Suite 400
Washington, D.C. 20001

Institute for the Advanced Study of Black Family Life &
   Culture
7700 Edgewater Drive Suite
Oakland, California 94621

National Black United Front
415 Atlantic Avenue
Brooklyn, New York 11217

National Council for Black Family & Child Development
P.O. Box 1204 Main Station
White Plains, New York

National Institute for Women of Color
1712 N Street N.W.
Washington, D.C. 20036

United Negro College Fund, Inc.
500 East 62nd Street
New York, NY 10021

Wilma Rudolph Foundation
850 North Meridian Street
Indianapolis, IN 46204

National Urban League
Youth Development Program
500 East 62nd Street
New York, NY

Black Child Journal
1426 East 49th Street
Chicago, IL 60615

Sisterhood of Black Single Mothers
1360 Fulton Street Suite 423
Brooklyn, NY 11216

IV. Educational Resources for Black Youth

The following educational resources can be used to assist in the positive development of Black youth:

An Afrocentric Educational Manual: Toward A Non-Deficit Perspective in Services to Families and Children, Jualynee E. Dodson, Atlanta University School of Social Work.

A Model for Developing Programs for Black Children, Black Child Development Institute, Inc. 1463 Rhode Island Avenue, N.W. Washington, D.C. 20005.

A Non-Racist Framework for the Analysis of Educational Programs for Black Children, Margaret King. R&E Research Associates, Inc., 936 Industrial Avenue, Palo Alto, California 94303.

Educational Alternatives for Colonized People Models for Liberation, Robert L. Williams. Dunellen, New York.

A Guidebook for Planning Alcohol Presentation Programs with Black Youth, U.S. Department of Health & Human Services, Washington, D.C.

Working With Teen Parents: A Survey of Promising Approaches, Family Resource Coalition, Chicago, Illinois.

Challenges: A Young Man's Journal for Self-Awareness and Personal Planning, Advocacy Press, Santa Barbara, California.

Programs for Preadolescents.

Programs for Young Men.

Peer Education Programs, Center for Population Options, 2031 Florida Avenue, Washington, D.C.

A Resource Guide on Black Children and Youth, Institute for Urban Affairs & Research, Howard University, Washington, D.C.

Portrait of Inequality: Black and White Children in America, *America's Children and Their Families: Key Facts*, Children's Defense Fund, 1520 New Hampshire Avenue, N.W., Washington, D.C. 20036.

The Resource Guide, Ben Johnson, Washington, D.C.

V. Resource Books on Black Youth

The following books deal with problems which are particularly relevant to Black youth:

Home Is A Dirty Street: The Social Oppression of Black Children, Useni Eugene Perkins. Third World Press, Chicago, Illinois.

Black Youth in Crisis, Ernest Cashmere. George Allen, Boston, Massachusetts.

Hustling and Other Hard Work Life Styles in the Ghetto, Betty Lou Valentine. The Free Press, New York, New York.

The Black Underclass: Poverty, Unemployment and Entrapment of Ghetto Youth, Douglas G. Glasgow. Vintage Books, New York.

Different Strokes: Pathways to Maturity in the Boston Ghetto, Ford Foundation Report. Westview Press, Boulder, Colorado.

Black Children: Their Roots, Culture and Learning Styles, Janice E. Hale. Brigham Young University Press.

Countering The Conspiracy to Destroy Black Boys, Jawanza Kunjufu. Afro-Am Publishing Co., Chicago, Illinois.

Image Of A Man, Michael Brown. East Publications, Brooklyn, New York.

Developing Masculinity: The Black Male's Role in American Society, Robert Staples. Black Scholar Press.

Tomorrow's Tomorrow: The Black Woman, Joyce A. Ladner. Anchor Books, Garden City, New York.

The Developmental Psychology of the Black Child, Amos N. Wilson. Africana Research Publications, New York, New York.

Black Children Just Keep On Growing Alternative Curriculum Models for Young Black Children, Black Child Development Institute.

The Survival of Black Children & Youth, National Council for Black Child Development, Nuclassics and Science Publishing Co., Washington, D.C.

Children of Bondage: The Personality of Negro Youth In the Urban South, Allison Davis and John Dollard.

Negro Youth at the Crossways: Their Personality Development in the Middle States, E. Franklin Frazier.

Growing Up In The Black Belt: Negro Youth in the Rural South, Charles Johnson.

Dating Habits of Young Black Americans, John Porter. Kendall/Hunt Publishing, Co., Dubuque, Iowa 52001.

Growing Up (Sex Education), Dr. James Docherty, Lika Publishing Foundation, Lagos, Nigeria.

Transformation: Rites of Passage Manual For African American Girls, Moore, Gilyard, King-McCreary, Warfield-Coppack, Stars Press, New York.

CHARACTERISTICS OF BLACK YOUTH
CONCERNS AND PROBLEMS

		Black	White
1.	Infant Mortality Rate (per thousand births)	21.1	12.0
2.	Percent of Children with Mother in the Labor Force		
	Under 6 years	51.4	41.5
	Under 18 years	57.4	52.0
3.	Percent of Children under 18 years Old who Live in Households Under the Poverty Level		
	Metropolitan	38.1	10.4
	Inside Central Cities	41.9	15.7
	Outside Central Cities	28.3	7.9
	Nonmetropolitan Areas	48.7	13.3
	North and West	36.7	10.7
	South	44.2	13.0
4.	Persons Under 14 Years Old (Numbers in thousands)	7,349	38,013
5.	Persons 14 to 24 Years Old (Numbers in thousands)	6,213	38,130
6.	Children 3-5 years old enrolled in Nursery School or Kindergarten	51.0	52.7
7.	School Enrollment of Persons 6-25 years old (Number in thousands)		
	Ages 6-13	99.3	99.2
	Ages 14-17	94.2	93.4
	Ages 18-24	34.7	38.7
	Ages 22-24	13.7	16.3
8.	High School Graduates	69.7	82.5
9.	College Enrollment	27.8	32.0
10.	Death Rates for Persons 1-24 years old (per 1,000)		
	Ages 1-4	0.9	0.5
	Ages 5-14	0.4	0.3
	Ages 15-24	1.4	1.1
11.	Percentage of Children living with both Parents (1978)	49.4	85.7
12.	Percentage of High School Dropouts among Persons 14-34 years old (1977)	20.0	12.4
13.	Black Male Suicide Rates (per 100,000 persons) 1977		
	Ages 20-24	21.5	—
	Ages 25-29	28.5	—

Most of the above data was taken from *Characteristics of American Children and Youth*, 1980, Bureau of the Census.

EPILOGUE

Rise Black Youth!

a new harvest
must be planted
to help future generations
blossom into adulthood
with values and knowledge
which liberate their minds
from the shackles of oppression
and the social diseases
that contaminate their lives

> Rise Black youth!
> take hold of your roots
> Rise Black youth!
> take control of your present

a new harvest
must be cultivated
so Black youth can fulfill
their true potential
and become the energizers
for preserving Black traditions
raising strong families
developing positive images
and building Black institutions

> Rise Black youth!
> take hold of your identity
> Rise Black youth!
> take control of your minds

a new harvest
must be sowed
that germinates
from our African vestiges
and embodies the wisdom
of our ancestors
to prepare Black youth
for their Rites of Passage
and ascension to adulthood

> Rise Black youth!
> take hold of your lives
> Rise Black youth!
> Take command of your destiny

ALSO AVAILABLE FROM THIRD WORLD PRESS

Nonfiction

The Destruction Of Black Civilization: Great Issues Of A Race From 4500 B.C. To 2000 A.D.
by Dr. Chancellor Williams
paper $16.95
cloth $29.95

The Cultural Unity Of Black Africa
by Cheikh Anta Diop $14.95

Home Is A Dirty Street
by Useni Eugene Perkins $9.95

Black Men: Obsolete, Single, Dangerous?
by Haki R. Madhubuti
paper $14.95
cloth $29.95

From Plan To Planet Life Studies: The Need For Afrikan Minds And Institutions
by Haki R. Madhubuti $7.95

Enemies: The Clash Of Races
by Haki R. Madhubuti $12.95

Kwanzaa: A Progressive And Uplifting African-American Holiday
by Institute of Positive Education
Intro. by Haki R. Madhubuti $2.50

Harvesting New Generations: The Positive Development Of Black Youth
by Useni Eugene Perkins $12.95

Explosion Of Chicago Black Street Gangs
by Useni Eugene Perkins $6.95

The Psychopathic Racial Personality And Other Essays
by Dr. Bobby E. Wright $5.95

Black Women, Feminism And Black Liberation: Which Way?
by Vivian V. Gordon $5.95

Black Rituals
by Sterling Plumpp $8.95

The Redemption Of Africa And Black Religion
by St. Clair Drake $6.95

How I Wrote Jubilee
by Margaret Walker $1.50

A Lonely Place Against The Sky
by Dorothy Palmer Smith $7.95

Fiction

Mostly Womenfolk And A Man Or Two: A Collection
by Mignon Holland Anderson $5.95

The Brass Bed and Other Stories
Pearl Cleage $8.00

Poetry and Drama

To Disembark
by Gwendolyn Brooks $6.95

I've Been A Woman
by Sonia Sanchez $7.95

My One Good Nerve
by Ruby Dee $8.95

Geechies
by Gregory Millard $5.95

Earthquakes And Sunrise Missions
by Haki R. Madhubuti $8.95

Killing Memory: Seeking Ancestors
(Lotus Press)
by Haki R. Madhubuti $8.00

Say That The River Turns:
The Impact Of Gwendolyn Brooks
(Anthology)
Ed.by Haki R. Madhubuti $8.95

Octavia And Other Poems
by Naomi Long Madgett $8.00

A Move Further South
by Ruth Garnett $7.95

Manish
by Alfred Woods $8.00

New Plays for the Black Theatre
(Anthology)
edited by Woodie King, Jr. $14.95

Wings Will Not Be Broken
Darryl Holmes $8.00

Sortilege (Black Mystery)
by Abdias do Nascimento $2.95

Children's Books
The Day They Stole
The Letter J
by Jabari Mahiri $3.95

The Tiger Who Wore
White Gloves
by Gwendolyn Brooks $5.00

A Sound Investment
by Sonia Sanchez $2.95

I Look At Me
by Mari Evans $2.50

The Story of Kwanzaa
by Safisha Madhubuti $5.95

Black Books Bulletin
A limited number of back issues
of this unique journal are available
at $3.00 each:

Vol. 1, Fall '71   Interview with
                  Hoyt W. Fuller

Vol. 1, No. 3   Interview with
                  Lerone Bennett, Jr.

Vol. 5, No. 3   Science & Struggle

Vol. 5, No. 4   Blacks & Jews

Vol. 7, No. 3   The South

Order from **Third World Press**
7524 S. Cottage Grove Ave.
Chicago, IL 60619

Shipping: Add $2.00 for first book
and .25 for each additional book.
Mastercard /Visa orders may be placed
by calling 1(312) 651-0700